Local Tax Policy in Central and Eastern Europe

This book navigates the complexities of local real estate taxation in the dynamic region of Central and Eastern Europe, providing a meticulous analysis of the diverse approaches taken across the region. From Poland to Hungary, Romania to the Czech Republic, this book explores the historical roots and evolution of local real estate tax, its importance in municipal fiscal policy and its impact on communities.

This book analyses the motives and models used by municipal authorities in their calculations around real estate tax and considers whether they are primarily a fiscal tool, related to budget revenues, or stimulants for future growth aimed at boosting local socio-economic development. It also explores whether municipalities compete with neighbouring entities on taxation and the extent to which the political cycle and the meeting of voter demands and expectations play a role.

This book will be of great interest to readers in public economics and finance, taxation policy and law, local government and the CEE region more broadly.

Paweł Felis is habilitated Doctor of Economic Sciences in the Discipline of Finance and Associate Professor at the Institute of Finance of the SGH Warsaw School of Economics.

Leszek Patrzałek is Full Professor of Economic Sciences in Economics and Finance.

Agnieszka Bem is habilitated Doctor of Economic Sciences in the Discipline of Finance and Associate Professor at the Department of Corporate and Public Finance.

Michał Bernardelli is habilitated Doctor, Associate Professor at the SGH Warsaw School of Economics, and Dean of Graduate Studies at the SGH Warsaw School of Economics.

Elżbieta Malinowska-Misiąg has a PhD in Economics and works at the Financial System Department of the Warsaw School of Economics.

Jarosław Olejniczak is Assistant Professor at the Finance Department at the Wroclaw University of Economics and Business (Poland) and has a PhD in Economics.

Milena Kowalska has a PhD in Economics and Finance, works at the Department of Corporate and Public Finance at the Wroclaw University of Economics and Business.

Routledge Research in Taxation

About the Series

From suggestions for taxing carbon, tech companies and wealth, to methods for reducing avoidance, and questions of justice and fairness, taxation issues are at the core of discussions around the future shape of the economy. In this light, the 'Routledge Research in Taxation' series provides a home for cutting-edge and interdisciplinary research on all aspects of tax and its impact on individuals, corporations and government. The series comprises monographs and edited volumes drawing on insights from a wide range of perspectives including accounting, anthropology, business ethics, corporate social responsibility, economic psychology, law, philosophy, political economy and sociology.

For more information about this series, please visit: https://www.routledge.com/Routledge-Research-in-Taxation/book-series/RRIT

Local Tax Policy in Central and Eastern Europe

Property Taxation and Municipal Finance

Paweł Felis, Leszek Patrzałek, Agnieszka Bem, Michał Bernardelli, Elżbieta Malinowska-Misiąg, Jarosław Olejniczak and Milena Kowalska

Ministry of Science and Higher Education
Republic of Poland

SGH
Warsaw School of Economics

Wroclaw
UNIVERSITY OF ECONOMICS AND BUSINESS

Routledge
Taylor & Francis Group
LONDON AND NEW YORK

First published 2025
by Routledge
4 Park Square, Milton Park, Abingdon, Oxon OX14 4RN

and by Routledge
605 Third Avenue, New York, NY 10158

Routledge is an imprint of the Taylor & Francis Group, an informa business

The project is co-financed by the state budget, granted by the Minister of Education and Science under the Excellent Science II Programme - Support for scientific monographs.

The monograph is the result of research conducted as part of the second edition of the SGH-UEW Intercollegiate Research Grant implemented in 2020–2023.

British Library Cataloguing-in-Publication Data
A catalogue record for this book is available from the British Library

ISBN: 978-1-032-86939-1 (hbk)
ISBN: 978-1-032-87023-6 (pbk)
ISBN: 978-1-003-53050-3 (ebk)

DOI: 10.4324/9781003530503

Typeset in Times New Roman
by codeMantra

Contents

Figures

Tables

About the Authors

Paweł Felis: habilitated doctor of economic sciences in the discipline of finance and Associate Professor at the Institute of Finance of the SGH Warsaw School of Economics; deals with the issues of finance and corporate taxation as well as the theory and practice of wealth taxes; a coordinator and participant of projects related, for instance, to real property taxation within local tax policies or greening of the tax system; the author and co-author of about 150 scientific and informative publications, as well as opinions and expert reports for the Chancellery of the Sejm of the Republic of Poland.

Leszek Patrzałek: Full Professor of economic sciences in economics and finance. Her research interests include public finance, in particular, the finances of local government units. The author of over 200 scientific publications, member of the Committee on Financial Sciences of the Polish Academy of Sciences, and member of the College of the Regional Audit Chamber in Wrocław in 2011–2013.

Agnieszka Bem: habilitated doctor of economic sciences in the discipline of finance and Associate Professor at the Department of Corporate and Public Finance; deals with the issues of public finance, corporate finance, and health economics. The author and co-author of about 160 scientific publications. The member of the Polish Economic Society and the Scientific Board of Small and SME Spokesman.

Michał Bernardelli: habilitated doctor, Associate Professor at the SGH Warsaw School of Economics, and Dean of Graduate Studies at the SGH Warsaw School of Economics. He holds a degree in mathematics and computer science from the Faculty of Mathematics, Computer Science and Mechanics of the University of Warsaw, where he also earned his doctoral degree in applied mathematics. He received his postdoctoral degree in economic sciences at the SGH Warsaw School of Economics. A consultant and contractor for many scientific and commercial projects, including the Ministry of Finance, Education and Science, and the National Bank of Poland.

Elżbieta Malinowska-Misiąg: PhD in economics. Works at the Financial System Department of the Warsaw School of Economics. In 2006–2007, she was also an advisor to the Minister of Finance. She is an author or co-author of several dozen studies and publications, as well as numerous reports and expert opinions in the area of public finance, including for the Polish Parliament, Ministry of Finance, and Ministry of Regional Development. Her scientific and research interests include, among others, institutional aspects of general government, fiscal transparency, and local government financing.

Jarosław Olejniczak: Assistant Professor at the Finance Department at the Wroclaw University of Economics and Business (Poland). PhD in economics. An expert in the field of public finances. Researcher, lecturer, certified trainer and consultant. Author of over 90 articles and conference publications and co-author in several monographs. His scientific work mainly deals with local government finance issues (tax policy, equalisation schemes), local and regional sustainable development, and citizen participation in local government activities. A member of the Global Participatory Budgeting Research Board at PeoplePowered.Org, the International Institute of Public Finance, and the Senate of the Wroclaw University of Economics and Business.

Milena Kowalska: Has a PhD in Economics and Finance, works at the Department of Corporate and Public Finance at the Wroclaw University of Economics and Business. Researcher, lecturer, certified trainer, and consultant. An expert in the field of public finances. Businesswomen and a city councilwoman. The research areas are public finance and basic income – a member of The Basic Income Earth Network.

Acknowledgements

The project is co-financed by the state budget, granted by the Minister of Education and Science under the Excellent Science II Programme – Support for scientific monographs.

The monograph is the result of research conducted as part of the second edition of the SGH-UEW Intercollegiate Research Grant implemented in 2020–2023.

Introduction

Apart from the value-based property tax systems typical of the decisive majority of EU countries, Europe also has area-based and mixed systems, which, in principle, occur in particular Central and Eastern European states. The tax base for the real property tax may be expressed in terms of quantity (based on specific external features, such as the surface area recorded in the land register, and therefore independent of their market value) or value (based on a method of evaluation adopted in commercial transactions).

As a critical local tax, real property tax is an essential feature of the local government system. After all, municipality authorities can influence the development of sources that generate such revenues and structure their amounts. Most often, however, real property tax is related to the so-called limited taxing power. In Poland, for example, this power is determined on the one hand by the constitutional principle claiming that taxes are imposed by the parliament and on the other by granting municipalities the right to determine the amount of tax within their statutory scope. In the case of the real property tax, the taxing power of municipalities is manifested in the ability to affect the tax structure by lowering and differentiating tax rates and introducing tax exemptions.

The monograph scope concerns real property taxation systems employed primarily in the Central and Eastern European countries. The empirical analysis is based on the example of the Czech, Polish, Romanian, Slovak, and Hungarian experiences of local governments in real property taxation. Due to the availability of detailed empirical data and the possibility of conducting more in-depth research, special attention is paid to local units in Poland. Let us emphasise that most of the published studies are limited in scope. In most European countries, the importance of real property tax in municipal budgets is much lower than in Poland. The theoretical and empirical considerations aim to fill the existing state-of-the-art gap in real property taxation models and their impact on local government finances. Our monograph includes a few comprehensive elaborations in which the studies on local tax policies employed in selective research of other countries refer to theoretical concepts.

This monograph brings added value to the development of knowledge in various areas of local government finance. Given the lack of European

DOI: 10.4324/9781003530503-1

studies, the knowledge gap regarding tax policy at the local level is bridged. First, we included comprehensive theoretical examinations of local tax policy in the real property tax field. Moreover, we discussed the determinants affecting the fiscal capacity of real property tax in selected countries in Central and Eastern Europe. Most importantly, what is innovative in the work is the analysis that examines the motives of municipal tax policy. It is the only study that addresses the issue of local tax policy in such a comprehensive way, using the example of a country where the significance of real property tax and the freedom to set it are among the greatest in Europe.

The cognitive aim of the monograph is to identify and explain the motives behind the decisions made by municipalities in the field of real property tax. We refer to an important question: What are the motives for the decisions made by the authorities regarding the amount of real property tax? Fiscal: Are they concerned with current and future budget revenues? Stimulus: Are they related to boosting local socio-economic development and competing with neighbouring municipalities in taxation? Or it could be about the political determinants of the decisions made (the political cycle, meeting voters' expectations). The answer to these questions requires in-depth studies of local tax policy.

The empirical aims of the monograph are:

1 Assessment of the degree of differentiation of local tax policies.
2 Evaluation of the effects of property tax rate reductions.
3 Investigating the willingness of municipalities to compete for the tax base (the phenomenon of tax competition).

The study goals and scopes determined the selected and applied methodology. In the theoretical part, methods include a literature review, descriptive analysis, interpretation, and inference. The empirical section employed quantitative and qualitative approaches based on diverse factual data from sources like Eurostat and national finance ministries. Essential analytical tools include descriptive statistics and correlation analysis, with aggregations presented through tabular summaries and visualisations of cross-sectional data and time series. The significance of the relationship was checked with statistical tests.

This monograph results from studies conducted as part of the second edition of the SGH-UEW Inter-University Research Grant implemented in 2020–2022.[1] It includes an introduction, four chapters, a summary, and an annexe. The first two chapters are theoretical, and the other two present the results of our original research.

Below, we provide a detailed discussion of the content of all chapters. The initial chapter serves as a starting point for subsequent thorough analyses. Its primary objective is to provide a theoretical framework for understanding local tax policy, focusing on real property taxation. This section highlights its scope, types and objectives. A lot of space is devoted to presenting theoretical concepts (tax competition, the concept of the average voter, the political electoral cycle and the party model, and political budget cycles). Moreover, this chapter synthesises critical insights from global research on local tax policy.

The second chapter delves into the essential aspects of property tax theory. It begins by discussing the impact of real property tax within specific theoretical frameworks, considering economic considerations. The text identifies unique features of this tax, highlighting its status as one of the most prevalent local taxes worldwide. The focus is on understanding the distinct attributes of local real property tax within the realm of tax policy, emphasising its essential characteristics about policy objectives.

The third chapter discusses real property taxation in Central and Eastern European countries, namely Czechia, Hungary, Poland, Romania, and Slovakia, where area-based tax predominates. The chapter's initial section explains property tax fiscal significance and its crucial role as a revenue source for local budgets. It examines the endogenic determinants affecting the fiscal effectiveness of real property tax, analysing its critical structural components with a particular focus on observed disparities in the reviewed countries. The potential transition of the area-based tax to the value-based system is also explored. Subsequently, the chapter investigates the factors affecting the fiscal capacity of taxes, which are set by local authorities. Drawing upon research from various countries and utilising data, particularly from Poland, where property tax is of principal importance, this section offers a comprehensive analysis of the determinants shaping the tax fiscal capacity.

In the fourth chapter of the research, an attempt is made to identify and explain in detail the reasons behind tax decisions made by municipalities in Poland. The chapter refers to various theoretical concepts of local tax policy mentioned in the first chapter, such as tax competition, the idea of the average voter, the political cycle, the party model, fiscal motive, and the possibility of stimulating local socio-economic development. The research takes a holistic approach to the real property tax issue, including quantitative analyses of questionnaire responses, data from the Ministry of Finance, and qualitative studies based on focus groups.

The publication is addressed to the academic world and representatives of local communities. The reflections in the monograph can be used as substantive support for those dealing with local finance in practice. The work may also inspire researchers to conduct further theoretical and empirical research on local tax policy and European countries' real property taxation systems.

Note

1 A study entitled: *The policy of Polish municipality governments concerning real property taxation.* The research team consisted of Paweł Felis, Professor

of SGH (project leader); Prof. Leszek Patrzałek; Agnieszka Bem, Professor of the Wrocław University of Economics; Michał Bernardelli, Professor of SGH; Elżbieta Malinowska-Misiąg, PhD; Jarosław Olejniczak, PhD and Milena Kowalska. The monograph was recognised by the Minister of Education and Science as part of the Excellent Science II programme – support for academic monographs.

1 Local tax policy as part of a municipality's financial policy

1.1 The essence and objectives of local tax policy

The financial policy of a municipality, understood in general terms as the activities of local government bodies consisting of determining and attempting to achieve specific objectives through the totality of financial operations, requires the local government authorities to define a hierarchy of goals, methods, and instruments used to implement such objectives. In terms of achieving the set objectives, the process in which municipality bodies design and make decisions on internally consistent activities projected over several years and related to collecting and disbursing financial resources is a complex process encompassing several areas, each of which has a specific nature that is expressed in their object and the instruments used by local government bodies. One such area includes events and processes related to the influx of revenue from local taxes to the municipality budget.

The fiscal federalism theory, which is one of the main economic concepts that refers to the idea of multi-level public finances (more: Musgrave 1959; Buchanan 1960), assumes that municipalities have a defined scope of *local tax autonomy,* which is a condition that must be met before a local tax policy can appear and be implemented (see: Blöchliger 2013, 81). It can be argued that in contemporary social systems operating under democratic principles and market conditions, the entity responsible for the entirety of matters related to the part of the financial resources of local communities derived from local taxes is the municipality. As a public law entity, the municipality, therefore, pursues a local tax policy that can be defined as the activity of municipality bodies consisting of decisions on how to use local taxes to achieve specific goals.[1]

These are universal objectives, including fiscal objectives related to the demand for money signalled by the municipality and the provision of revenue from local taxes and non-fiscal objectives related to influencing and stimulating economic and social development processes by municipality bodies.

Local tax policy also has specific objectives, which differ for each municipality. As a public law entity, the municipality government is not restricted to

DOI: 10.4324/9781003530503-2

the public utility sphere. It uses local taxes to influence the activity of entities operating in the municipality to solve specific economic and social problems found in the area.

One of the essential components of the municipality development strategy is the tax policy of local government authorities, which is supposed to offer advantages over other competing locations that can be used to settle down and establish enterprises. For this reason, when determining local tax rates, municipality bodies consider the tax policy of adjacent municipalities or the level of affluence of residents. In addition, local government authorities undertake actions to improve their ability to collect due local taxes (see Patrzałek 1994).

While pursuing their local tax policy, municipalities tend to secure a level of revenue that will provide sufficient financing for the public goods they supply, enhance the municipality's competitiveness, and procure conditions for economic and social development on the local level.

In times of globalisation, openness of contemporary economies, and free movement of goods and services, local tax policy must increasingly account for fiscal competition and the related diversity in budgetary consequences of a municipality's tax policy (more: Felis and Otczyk 2021). Municipalities compete for investors and taxpayers, and therefore, achieving local tax policy objectives to enhance a municipality's competitiveness involves using tax instruments and introducing changes in tax charges depending on the local economic and social situation. Since each municipality has its own independent revenue, local tax rates in Poland are varied, and local government authorities make choices concerning the level and quality of public services provided while considering the specific circumstances and preferences of members of the local community. This fosters competition between individual municipalities that offer varied scopes and levels of public services. The different costs of provided services consequently determine the rates of local taxes imposed on natural persons residing and legal persons operating in the area of a particular basic territorial unit.

The municipality considers the effectiveness of tax instruments, considering the motives and conditions of investors and manufacturers' activities, focusing on dependencies between the taxation scale, size of economic activities, and the level of achieved tax revenue. The type and nature of local tax policy pursued by municipality bodies is one of the components taken into consideration by businesses when making various decisions, for example, concerning the location of their investments, the sources of their financing, and suppliers and outlets. Entrepreneurs who can function under various tax designs will look for the most favourable ones. Accordingly, businesses may make specific decisions while considering the nature and kind of tax policy pursued by municipality bodies.

The factors that largely determine the implementation of local tax policy can be divided into internal factors dependent (in a specific scope) on municipality bodies and external factors independent of them.

Internal factors include, among others, the municipality's revenue generation ability, which means achieving revenue from its sources. The pattern of tax revenue mainly influences this ability. Other factors include, among others, geographical and environmental factors, demographic factors, forms of dialogue between the local community and municipality bodies, and the level and dynamics of the municipality's economic and social development.

External factors include, among others, the structure of local taxes, limitations related to the state's fiscal policy, and possible projections of municipality budget revenue. The total municipality budget revenue is primarily the result of statutory regulations or decisions made by governmental institutions. Among other external factors are macroeconomic factors, fiscal relations between the state and local government, and the legal status of the finance system used by local government authorities.

1.2 Scope and types of local tax policy

The local tax policy is determined mainly by the extent of the tax-related powers of the municipality. Enjoying full tax-related powers, which consist of municipality bodies being granted competencies to affect the design of particular components of the local tax structure, contributes to the greater responsibility of municipal authorities (concerning members of local communities) for the economic and social development of the municipality and also to their broader independence in achieving revenue. Limited tax-related powers of the municipality, in turn, allow it to affect only specific components of the local tax structure, meaning that municipal bodies are, to a large extent, limited in independently obtaining and collecting revenue from local taxes and their ability to affect the processes of economic and social development by using tax instruments is low. In practice, many countries have adopted an intermediate solution that results in limited tax-related powers of the municipality, with the extent of such limitation being a key topic open to debate.

In these reflections, it is essential to consider the features of taxes that feed into the municipality budget. Most frequently, among the tax revenue of a municipality budget, one may distinguish taxes affected by tax-related powers to varying extents. This extent of tax-related powers applies not only to the competence to influence the components of tax structure but also to enacting provisions of law related to collecting and administering revenue from specific taxes. When the municipality bodies are the entities authorised to establish any tax charges on the municipality area, such sources of tax revenues for the municipality budget are classified as self-standing local government taxes. The above group of local taxes occurs to a minimal extent in the local government finance systems of individual states (more: Piotrowska-Marczak 2009), which is primarily due to political (public opinion) but also procedural (costs of introducing a tax) reasons. In addition, it needs to be stressed that introducing such taxes may lead to more profound differences and imbalances in the territorial of municipalities' revenue.

Local taxes are the principal source of tax revenue for municipality budgets worldwide. This revenue belongs entirely to the municipality budget, and municipality bodies enjoy a specific extent of tax-related powers concerning them. They differ from self-standing local government taxes in that they are introduced uniformly on the territory of the entire state and not by a decision of a municipality body. Local taxes are characterised by the following:

- municipal bodies enjoy exclusive use of all revenue generated by the tax;
- by decision of state authorities, they have been handed over to the municipalities for an undefined period (indefinitely);
- municipal bodies have the competencies to independently affect the components of the tax structure, although it must be stressed that such competencies may vary considerably (e.g. tax rates, credits, and exemptions) – the deciding factors are political considerations and the constitutional system prevailing in a particular country, which dictates the degree and extent of decentralisation;
- the tax charge applies to tax subjects residing in the territory of a municipality and does not affect entities residing outside that territory;
- the object of taxation is permanently fixed in a specific location, which makes tax evasion essentially impossible.

Local municipal authorities have the right to impose taxes and determine their amounts, as well as the ability to apply specific tax preferences, thereby pursuing their local tax policy. Subject literature (Swianiewicz 1996, 75–80) distinguishes the following kinds of tax policy:

- liberal policy, in which tax rates are relatively low. This municipal tax policy is based on the principles of liberalism and the belief that each intervention of municipal bodies in the economic and social sphere may lead to distortion of the market mechanism and ineffective management of public resources. Such local tax policy assumes that the use of tax instruments by municipal bodies to influence economic and social development is ineffective and that market mechanisms play the dominant role in the development of the municipality;
- stimulating policy, which assumes a wide-ranging intervention of municipal bodies. In local development concepts that incorporate the theoretical foundations of interventionism, an assumption is made that different municipalities develop differently and that such differences must be overcome through the intervention of municipal bodies that use tax instruments. On the one hand, local government interventions focus on making local public services available and, on the other, on influencing the economic activity of entities in specific basic territorial division units. By launching interventions and setting the amounts of local tax rates, exemptions, and

credits, municipal bodies focus primarily on undertakings that promote development based on the municipality's resources and capabilities;
- populist policy, which is characterised by low tax rates for the majority of residents, in contrast to higher tax rates affecting small groups of taxpayers. The idea of this policy is based on assumptions of the public choice theory in which light the actions of municipal authorities focus solely on representing and recognising opinions expressed by voters;
- fiscal policy, in which the rates of all local taxes are high. Such policy leads to increasing the revenue of municipality budgets. From a long-term perspective, excessive fiscalism may cause a drop in tax revenue, as taxpayers exhibit diverse reactions to growing tax charges.

In Poland, the Constitution of the Republic of Poland indicates that taxes and other public fees are imposed using an act (1997 art. 217). It should also be noted that the adopted solution is not contrary to the provisions of the European Charter of Local Self-Government (more in EKSL 1994), which stipulates, among others, that at least part of the financial resources of local authorities should be derived from local taxes and charges of which those communities have the power to determine the rate within limits of the statute. Taking tax-related powers into account, taxes in the revenue pattern of municipality budgets may be divided into two groups: taxes with limited municipal tax-related powers (real estate tax, transport vehicles tax, agricultural tax, and forest tax) and taxes over which the municipal council has no tax-related powers whatsoever (civil law transactions tax, inheritances, and donations tax).

The limited extent of tax-related powers of Polish municipalities has a decisive influence on the ability to conduct local tax policy. From the viewpoint of the present discussions, which refer to connections between the municipal tax policy and local development, including the real estate market development on a particular territory, the stimulating tax policy appears to be a reasonable choice for municipalities. Questions arise, however, about the extent and possibility of pursuing such a policy and its effectiveness in the finance system applicable to Polish local governments. Subject literature often stresses that the system is poorly suited to contemporary economic and social conditions and the position of local government in the public finance sector (Poniatowicz 2015; Famulska et al. 2019; Felis et al. 2020). Accordingly, necessary reforms have been proposed that would, among others, widen the extent of tax-related powers of municipalities, which are a crucial factor determining their financial independence.

1.3 Theoretical concepts of local tax policy

1.3.1 Tax competition

Globalisation trends have significantly influenced the appearance of tax competition, a process of rivalry between states regarding which fiscal policy they pursue to encourage as many investors as possible to deposit their capital in a country. Tax competition involves undertaking tax policy activities to make an area attractive to investors (Oręziak 2007).

The considerable number of entities that clash with each other will always lead to competition. Local government units that carry out a set of identical tasks to satisfy local communities' needs and act under conditions of limited access to public money are under pressure of tax competition (Walasik 2014).

Local tax competition is, therefore:

> rivalry between multiple local government authorities, whose object is securing access to public money resources derived mainly from the compulsory collection of taxes. Public money resources that are the object of competition include both centralised funds in the state budget, which are derived from the most fiscally efficient indirect taxes, and the exploitation of mobile (displaceable) sources of taxation, such as revenue from taxation of capital and work.
>
> (Walasik 2014)

The right of local governments to establish local tax policy means that the scope of tax competition between local government authorities depends on the power of local authorities to determine the level of taxes. The more extensive these powers, the broader the scope of such activities. Local tax competition may be understood to mean: "a situation in which the tax policy of a particular local government unit is altered in reaction (and taking into account) the policy pursued by neighbouring units or other local governments perceived as the principal competitors" (Łukomska and Swianiewicz 2015, 15). Tax competition may involve tax rates, credits and exemptions, and negotiations with specific taxpayers.

The local tax competition phenomenon was first identified and became an object of public debate in the 1950s. The issue was brought up by economist Charles M. Tiebout, whose model assumed that local government units compete and that such competition leads to optimisation of the amount and structure of offered public goods. The residents, as taxpayers, may choose a service supplier (local government unit) and can expect that the quality of services provided will be proportional to the taxes they pay. They prefer a local government as the optimal service supplier entails migrating to the respective local government community, a phenomenon called "foot voting". The migration of many residents to another municipality may pose a real risk of losing a significant part of local government revenue. Hence, the local government should react by providing more public goods of higher quality. The Tiebout model assumes that, with many local government units, residents will tend to settle in areas where the ratio between the taxes paid and the quality of public goods is optimal. According to this model, the more moneyed residents may wish to pay higher taxes in return for a higher quality of public services, and the reverse is valid for the poorer classes. For Tiebout, this mechanism allows the discovery of the preferences of inhabitants as part of democratic choices, permits to establish a competitive market of public goods, and is an additional argument in favour of decentralising the state because the possibility to choose the supplier exists on the local level only (Tiebout 1956).

When subject to criticism, Tiebout's model also reveals some weak points, among which the following can be enumerated (Poniatowicz and Wyszkowska 2014):

- the limited mobility of residents who, under conditions of globalisation, do not base their migration decisions so much on the quality of supplying one or more public goods;
- the limited knowledge of residents concerning public goods;
- the fact that not all local governments can supply specific public goods; some of these may be beyond their financial and organisational capabilities. Not every municipality will be able to build and maintain schools, kindergartens, or swimming pools;
- the model does not consider external effects that appear between local governments.

H. Blöchliger, on the other hand, believes that when taxpayers are not satisfied with the level of public services offered, they may behave in one of three ways. First, they may choose to move to another local government unit. Second, they may slack off efforts contributing to increased income and economic development of the taxpayer's business and the local government unit. The third option is an attempt at tax fraud to evade taxes (Blöchliger 2013, 77–94).

Whether tax competition will exist between local governments depends on the following factors (Swianiewicz and Łukomska 2016; Tiebout 1956):

- the extent to which local governments may decide tax rates. More extensive powers of local government units result in a higher probability that local tax competition will appear;
- in the case of taxes with a more mobile base, the probability of tax competition is higher. The state should decide on such taxes. For this reason, the tax pattern is essential;
- territorial divisions – the smaller the units a territory is divided into, the higher the probability of tax competition;
- tax competition is more likely to occur in smaller local government units, with economies more open to and dependent on external investors.

Activities related to local tax competition in municipalities may involve (Swianiewicz and Łukomska 2016, 5–29):

- determining tax rates on a level that is competitive compared to other local government units;

- granting credits or exemptions to specific groups of taxpayers;
- conducting negotiations with specific taxpayers that a municipality intends to attract, retain, or support.

H. Blöchliger (2013, 77–94) believes that local governments should be allowed to compete locally and given freedom in determining tax rates, with interventions of the state limited to introducing credits, exemptions, and remissions. Having reviewed the available literature, he points out that:

- tax competition applies more frequently to income taxes than real estate taxes or consumption taxes;
- smaller local governments are potentially more vulnerable to enterprises abandoning the local area and, therefore, are more willing to lower tax rates;
- more prosperous local governments offer lower tax rates, but these can be observed to become uniform over time, with a tendency instead to increase them;
- the activities of local governments related to granting credits, exemptions, or postponements target mainly industries and sectors with the most mobile tax base;
- local governments that decide to lower their tax rates as part of tax competition do not maximise their revenue. They should raise the rates to increase budget revenue rather than lower them.

However, tax competition may positively improve the effective allocation of resources in the economy (Oates and Schwab 1988). In the context of the public choice question, competition may bring increased prosperity by curtailing the expansion of the public sphere (Wilson 1999, 296), while lower inflows to the budget may also have negative consequences. Too low financing of the public sphere may lead to subsidising public goods and services on an unsatisfactory level (Tiebout 1956, 416–424). Another argument against tax competition is the "race to zero" effect that is crippling for local governments and may cause deficits in their budgets (Oates 1972).

In politics, competition may motivate authorities to spend their funds more effectively (Dafflon 2014). The remaining arguments against tax competition are as follows:

- establishing fictitious tax bases;
- increasing differences in level of development.

On the other hand, arguments in favour of tax competition include adjusting local government policy to residents' preferences, which may form an incentive towards a pro-development policy and serve as a tool to attract investors when the local government is not well-off. Tax competition also allows for innovations in tax policy (Swianiewicz and Łukomska 2016, 5–29).

Two main reasons for the presence of tax competition are cited. The first is the desire to extend the base of taxpayers on whom local charges are levied, thereby potentially increasing revenue in the unit's budget. The new base may result directly from low tax rates (for example, the transport vehicles tax) or appear as a consequence (an extended base of personal income tax taxpayers due to residents settling in response to a low real estate tax rate). The other motive concerns political capital and local government's willingness to maintain or increase their support among voters. Taxpayers are also voters, so tax policy decision-makers want to fulfil their expectations and thereby indirectly ensure their support in elections (Swianiewicz and Łukomska 2016, 5–29).

1.3.2 The concept of the average voter

D. Black proposed the concept of the average (median) voter in his 1948 article entitled *On the Rationale of Group Decision-making* (1948).

D. Black was the first to use analytical economic tools to describe the process of making electoral decisions, with his work considered to have heralded the era of modern public choice theory (Piwowarski 2014).

Black's median voter theory says that with one dimension of political space and two competing candidates (parties), their position will gravitate towards the position occupied by the median voter, as taking a median position maximises their chances to win (Black 1948; Batorski and Bartkowski 2003).

A. Downs used the theory proposed by Black to analyse competition between politicians. As a result, a significant fraction of decisions made by local governments is explained through the median voter concept, which assumes that decisions made by local politicians reflect residents' views (Swianiewicz and Łukomska 2016, 5–29).

According to this concept, the authority does not attempt to make important ideas a reality but instead struggles to capture votes and adjusts its policy to voters' opinions. Residents vote for candidates whose views they agree with the most. The candidates, in turn, make their decisions by calculating potential gains and losses in the electorate. As far as this political calculation is concerned, the optimal approach is to identify with views that reflect the median preferences of voters (Cunow et al., 2021).

A. Downs believes that political candidates (parties) are guided solely by their interests and that their actions are motivated purely by the desire to obtain money, prestige, and power from winning elections. Parties (candidates) pursue a policy of winning elections rather than winning elections to pursue a policy. In Downs' opinion, candidates (parties) follow a policy to maximise votes. This is the political counterpart of the maximum utility theory. A. Downs believes: "Governments continue spending until the marginal vote gain from expenditure equals the marginal vote loss from financing" (Downs 1957, 96–114).

Local governments' competence to create tax policy means facing the same challenges as state authorities. The authorities can influence the funds expended from the budget and the amount of collected taxes, thus continuing to increase local expenditures as long as the marginal gain in the form of extra votes is equal to the loss of voters who decide to no longer vote for a candidate due to raised taxes.

The preferences represented by voters hardly consider the relationship between the amount of budget expenditure and the amount of collected taxes. Therefore, securing the expected level of public spending without raising taxes may prove impossible (Łukomska and Swianiewicz 2015).

According to the median voter theory, each candidate running in the elections wants their programme and views aligned with voters' expectations as closely as possible. When the political debate is one-dimensional, the median voter theory assumes an equilibrium point exists in the game. Both candidates situate themselves in the middle, in the sweet spot of the median voter. As noted by D. Przybysz:

> If candidate A chooses another strategy than the sweet spot of the median voter, for example by situating themselves to the right of that spot, the competing candidate B may take advantage of this by situating themselves just to the left of that spot. In such cases, voters situated to the left of candidate B, and the majority of voters, will vote for candidate B.
>
> (Przybysz 2003)

1.3.3 The political electoral cycle and the partisan political model

We should initiate the discussion on theoretical models of political budget cycles (PBCs) in local governments by noting the evolution of theories on relationships between political decisions and the functioning of the economy. The fact that a relationship exists between actions undertaken by groups in power as a result of political considerations on the one hand and the business cycle and shaping of the widely understood budget policy (especially on the expenditure side) on the other may today appear evident for those who follow the political situation in multiple countries. Nevertheless, theories describing the *political business and budget cycles* did not develop until the 1970s. In this respect, it should be noted that the roots of this theory are supposed to lie in the views and publications of M. Kalecki (1943), who pointed to the potential emergence of the political business cycle as a consequence of state interventionism resulting from the pressure exerted by employers and employees on the ruling circles in subsequent phases of the business cycle.

Literature offers a uniform view of the essence of the political business cycle, which can be defined as influencing the course of the general business cycle (macroeconomic variables such as production, inflation, or unemployment) by politicians in office. In simple terms, it can be stated that these politicians will try to use fiscal and monetary policy instruments to improve their chances for re-election.

The following are commonly recognised as the five key topics on which individual political business cycle models are focused (Nordhaus 1989, 2):

- *voters*, in the context of factors influencing their political choices (reasons for elections, rationality, access to information about economic processes);
- *parties*, in the context of the adopted model of action (determination to win the elections or focusing on achieving programme objectives);
- *economic structure*, in the context of vulnerability to influences, the kinds of potential (effective) instruments, and decision-makers;
- the kinds and sources of *shocks/disturbances* for the economy and politics, as regards the consequences they have for political processes;
- *party competencies* in the context of efficient and complete implementation of electoral promises (as seen by the voters).

Studies on the essence of political business cycles may be divided into two main streams. The first is based on the classic (pure) political business cycle theory proposed by W. Nordhaus in his 1975 article entitled *The Political Business Cycle* (Nordhaus 1975). The basis for Nordhaus' theory was, on the one hand, the properties of the short-term Philips curve (a hypothesis concerning the relationship between inflation and employment levels) and, on the other, the assumption that political parties strive to maximise votes garnered in upcoming elections and thereby retain power. The cycle model Nordhaus described is opportunistic, as its central premise is that those in power temporarily stimulate the economy as the elections approach. The essential assumption here is that voters make their decisions taking into account the government's latest achievements (Nordhaus 1975, 171) and do not notice the relationship between its activities and the election date ("irrational voter"). This means that voters' expectations are adaptive – voters focus more on recent experiences/observations than those from the beginning of the term. At the same time, a retrospective assessment is assumed, ignoring the future effects of undertaken actions. It should be added that voters, from the perspective of this model, are homogeneous. The main area in which electoral support is captured is lowering unemployment (a situation preferred by voters) before elections due to state intervention. This, however, comes at the price of subsequent increased inflation (not expected by the voters) and the need to counteract it with a restrictive monetary policy that leads to increased unemployment. To summarise, using the opportunities to influence elections by governments adopting a suitable economic policy results in business cycles triggered by politics.

Nordhaus's assumptions are significantly simplified, leading to criticism and the emergence of alternative political business cycle models. Attempts to expand upon Nordhaus' theory were also made, including the proposals of T. Persson and G. Tabellini (1990, 2002) and of K. Rogoff and A. Sibert (1988), which introduced into the model a certain rationality of voters in making decisions, asymmetry of information, and assessment of competences of individual parties. This was primarily a response to charges that voters assess parties' actions retrospectively. In the Persson-Tabellini model, voters are guided by all available information about the state of the economy (inflation). However, the information they have on the competencies of politicians is delayed in time. The parties, on the other hand, are willing to stimulate the business cycle to appear competent. Competence is signalled to voters by expediting the pace of economic growth due to using instruments (monetary policy) available to the ruling circles. This, in turn, causes rational voters to vote for competent politicians (or parties) who, in their opinion, can efficiently govern the country.

On the other hand, in the model proposed by K. Rogoff and A. Sibert, the voter assessment model is expanded by differentiating the level of competence of each party (Rogoff and Sibert 1988, 2). Only the politicians themselves, however, are aware of their competencies. It should be stressed that in this model, governments are the more "competent" and the less financial resources necessary to carry out specific tasks they demand. Early in the term, a government sets the income (taxes) required to ensure the financing of its functions during the term, which is a point of reference for voters in subsequent assessments. As the elections approach, governing politicians with high competencies tend to pursue an expansionary fiscal policy (increasing expenditures and deficit), which triggers a political business cycle. The problem here, on the one hand, is the asymmetry of information available to the government and voters (the government has information about the state of the economy that reflects its "competencies" before the voters do, which may translate into manipulating information or taking action to consolidate the positive image of the ruling party) and, on the other, the limited possibility of opposition parties to "prove" their competences. Continuing the discussion on PBCs, K. Rogoff noted that incumbents may achieve similar effects without increasing the deficit. In his opinion, the growing support for the ruling party may result from switching expenditures from investments to transfers in the pre-election period (Rogoff 1990). Consequently, the altered structure of expenditure triggers the PBC. These two models are considered one of the foundations of *political budget cycles*.

The opportunistic political business cycle model has been opposed by an approach assuming that an ideological drive underlies party actions, which translates into decisions made by the government (*partisan political business cycle)*. This concept is believed to originate with D. Hibbs, who in 1977 published the final version of his article *Political Parties and Macroeconomic*

Policy (Hibbs 1977). Referring to Nordhaus' concept and based on researching the post-war economies of 12 highly developed countries, D. Hibbs concluded that ruling political parties try to be guided by ideological considerations while attempting to fulfil the needs/expectations of their voters. Consequently, their actions primarily aim not to retain power but to maintain the preferred levels of macroeconomic indicators (resulting from political orientation) during their terms by employing suitable fiscal and monetary policy tools. It should be noted that, unlike in the Nordhaus model, the voters here are supposed to be heterogeneous. D. Hibbs notes that the objectives chosen by left-wing parties (which represent less affluent voters and focus on lowering unemployment and faster economic growth) and their right-wing counterparts (which represent 'capital owners' and pursue restrictive economic policies to suppress inflation) will be different. Shifts in the economic policy conducted by the state occur only when the ruling party changes, purportedly in response to the effects of the economic policy of the former regime. In this model, voters are guided by political sympathies resulting from aligning their preferences with a party's programme, and their expectations tend to adapt over time.

Considering the impact of the political orientation of the power circles (or the system of values, views and objectives) on their actions concerning the local government fiscal policy, the 'policy-seeking party' concept cannot be ignored (Müller and Strøm 1999, 7). In this case, the main objective of the incumbents is (in theory) to carry out their proposals (electoral programme) thanks to the mandate they obtained, regardless of what happens at the next election. B. Le Maux indicates that in local governments, this will often refer to a 'citizen-candidate' being elected (Le Maux 2007). The candidate's attitude is determined, on the one hand, by the political views they identify with and want to pursue and, on the other, by their social and economic status, which is usually reflected in political opinions. Achieving predefined political objectives should provide that person with suitable "benefits" (Osborne and Slivinski 1996).

The final model in our literature review is based on a concept derived by A. Alesina (1987), which builds upon the model of Hibbs by positing the existence of rational voters. As in the sensible opportunistic political cycle model by Rogoff, A. Alesina assumed that the voter would be guided by individual preferences regarding the expected level of inflation and unemployment, resulting in choosing the party that offers the highest expected utility.

For Alesina's model described above, A. Alesina, N. Roubini and G. D. Cohen (1997) summarised the most important features and effects noted in the literature:

- if the assumptions of the opportunistic model were correct, then one to two years before the elections, strong economic growth (as a result of state intervention) would appear, and the election year would be characterised by unemployment dipping below average and a significant hike in inflation as the election date approaches. Then, following the elections, the economy would experience a slowdown and a long-term inflation drop. At the same time, the ruling party should be re-elected;

- in the case of the rational opportunistic model, they noted the short-term stimulation of the economy by those in power (using both expansive fiscal and monetary policies) just before the start of the electoral campaign and tightening of the fiscal and monetary policy after elections with no significant influence on the business cycle as a result. The re-election of the ruling party can be expected if economic growth and employment indicators in the election year are positive;
- in the case of the partisan (original) model, they looked at the expected long-term appearance of high inflation or unemployment levels, which depends on the political preferences of the ruling party before the elections and is the result of using fiscal and monetary policy instruments adjusted to party priorities;
- the rational partisan model would be proven correct by the short-term appearance of higher unemployment and lower inflation, or higher inflation and lower unemployment, in the post-election period, and long-term higher inflation if the left were in power rather than the right (the issue of the relationship between "party colours" and conducted fiscal and monetary policy will be discussed later in the chapter).

1.3.4 Political budget cycles

Attempts to empirically verify political models of the business cycle in individual countries did not confirm its existence. However, based on observing changes in the fiscal policy of governments around the election date in comparison with long-term trends (growth of government expenditures, lowering taxes), a thesis was put forward about the occurrence of "vote buying" (Bickers and Stein 1996; Drazen and Eslava 2006; Hoare 1983), described as the political budget cycle (Shi and Svensson 2003). As already noted, the causes and occurrences of this cycle appeared in the context of developing the political business cycle theory. The first axis of debate was the reflections, started by Rogoff, on the impact of the electoral cycle on fiscal policy and especially on the use of its specific instruments.

Analysing PBC models, M. Shi and J. Svensson (2003, 70) noted that they can be divided into two groups. The first is based on information asymmetry about politicians' competencies (sometimes described as the *adverse selection models*), and the second comprises *moral hazard models*.

In the model mentioned above by Rogoff, public goods supplied by the state may be of an "investment" or "consumption" nature. In the pre-election period, those in power will attempt to reduce expenditure on investments to finance consumption (for example, through transfers). At the same time, a tendency to lower taxes (and replace them with loans, whose effects are not felt by the voters) may appear. Both types of action are meant to prove that the governing party is competent. A fiscal illusion, therefore, misleads the voters, as some of the tax charges they would have to bear if the level of public goods supply was maintained are delayed.

The work mentioned above by M. Shi and J. Svensson (2006), which aimed to explain the differences in the scale of PBCs in various countries, modified Rogoff's assumptions. The essential feature of this model is still the ability of the ruling party to manipulate fiscal policy instruments to capture voters. Regardless of its competencies, the claim (unlike Rogoff) is that the government will be motivated to act due to *moral hazard*. The motivation will be greater, the more significant the expected benefits resulting from re-election. M. Shi and J. Svensson underline that some of the voters may see greater access to public goods due to actions undertaken by politicians (piling up obligations) as confirmation of the high competencies of the latter. In this model, the voters are not a homogeneous group because some of them will be aware of being manipulated (with access to suitable knowledge and information on actions of the government, including the amount of deficit and debt level) and others will base their assessment on limited information (usually information that applies to them directly, such as the amount of support, access to public services, etc.).

M. Shi and J. Svensson demonstrate that, as financial management transparency and country growth increase, the incentive to manipulate should weaken.

In another model proposed by A. Drazen and M. Eslav (2006, 2010), voters are divided into different segments (by geography, demography, sector, or other factors). In this model, the groups that benefit from manipulation are usually voters who "vacillate". In contrast, the costs of manipulation are borne by voters whose political preferences (and therefore willingness to vote for a party) make them uninteresting to the government. This model is frequently called the "pork barrel spending" model. The essential aspect here is that the ruling party's actions do not need to cause an increase in deficit and debt since the mechanism may shift funds between groups. Differentiating tax charges may be one of the instruments that can be used for this purpose (Khemani 2000, 32). Consequently, undecided voters observe the actions taken by the government and conclude whether keeping the ruling party in power will bring them more significant benefits in the future than having it replaced by another (Drazen and Eslava 2006). It also needs to be noted that in the case of local authority elections, we should assume that the political preferences of those in power are not visible (local politicians cannot be assigned "party colours"). This model is, in part, also a response to allegations of dominant fiscal conservatism of voters that runs contrary to the PBC idea. Shifting expenditure or tinkering with its structure without increasing the deficit may help ensure that dislike of "manipulating" politicians does not manifest in the pre-election period (Drazen and Eslava 2010; Enkelmann and Leibrecht 2013; Eslava 2005).

1.4 Local tax policy in empirical research

1.4.1 Local tax competition in empirical research

The interest in researching local tax competition can, to date, be observed mainly since the late 20th century. The objects of such research, both at the municipality level and elsewhere, were primarily countries such as the United States (Ladd 1992; Case 1993; Besley and Case 1995; Hendrick, Wu, and Jacob 2007; Agrawal 2015; Gentry et al. 2020) and Canada (Brett and Pinkse 2000; Mintz and Smart 2004; Rizzo 2010). The analysis dealt with tax competition in its classical form (*tax mimicking*) and competition for political capital (*tax yardstick*). The following review focuses on studying competition in its classical form.

The European tax competition study pioneers included B. Heyndels and J. Vuchelen (1998), who analysed this phenomenon in Belgian municipalities. Municipalities in Belgium (589) are small and act in a uniform institutional environment, favouring conducting research. The authors focused on the rates of the most essential municipality taxes, i.e. local income tax and local real estate tax, in the budget year 1991. The study confirmed that municipalities use the same rates as their neighbours or even areas further afield, with fewer similarities as the distance grows.

A similar study for Belgian municipalities, using a dynamic model that covered the years 1983–1997, was conducted by J. F. Richard, H. Tulkens, and M. Verdonck (2005). Interactions between municipalities observed by the authors were inversely proportional to distance and directly proportional to similarities between the units. For income tax, the critical factor was similarity in per capita income and, for real estate tax, similarity in population density. Using the dynamic model allowed the authors to assert that adjustments of tax rates take place slowly. In the case of income tax, the difference (due to interaction) between the used and preferred rates decreased by 10% per year, and in the case of real estate tax, by 6% per year. It was concluded that although the existence of tax competition between Belgian municipalities can be confirmed, its importance is minor.

The local tax competition in Belgium was also dealt with by S. van Parys and T. Verbeke (2006), whose study covered the years 1990–2004 and, as in the remaining cases, involved local income tax and local real estate tax rates. Interactions between tax rates in neighbouring municipalities and units located further afield but belonging to the same socio-economic class were observed. When income tax rates in municipalities with similar socio-economic characteristics were lowered, rates in similar areas also decreased. Moreover, such decreases applied to income tax and real estate tax (interdependent interaction). When municipalities with similar socio-economic characteristics lowered the real estate tax rate, a decrease of this tax rate was very likely to occur in other municipalities but unlikely to affect, by way of analogy, the income tax rate. Researchers explained the asymmetry of interaction by the greater importance of income tax rates.

The interactions between local tax rates set by neighbouring Belgian municipalities were also confirmed by the studies of H. Jayet and S. Paty (2006), while no such dependency was confirmed for the real estate tax. The authors also analysed the impact of differences on interactions between neighbouring units in various regions, noting that they were more vital in the Brussels area.

Numerous studies on tax competition were also conducted in other countries, including Germany and Switzerland. For example, S. Hauptmeier, F. Mittermaier, and J. Rincke (2009) analysed tax competition and public outlays in 1,100 Baden-Württemberg municipalities from 1998 to 2004. They observed that lowering economic activity tax rates by municipalities affected both the reduction of rates in other units and the increase of outlays for local infrastructure, which allowed the authors to state that municipalities react to competition in a somewhat flexible way and that taxes and public expenditure may be treated as alternative means to attract capital. Tax competition in Baden-Württemberg municipalities was also analysed by E. Janeba and S. Osterloh (2013) based on questionnaire surveys addressed to mayors in 2008. Tax competition for mobile capital proved more intense in larger urban centres than in smaller municipalities. In addition, such competition involves the immediate neighbours and other units located at a considerable distance in larger units. In 2020, interesting research results were published by T. Baskaran (2020), who studied tax competition between 158 eastern and 133 Western municipalities located along the border formerly dividing the Federal Republic of Germany and the German Democratic Republic. The author demonstrated that East German municipalities mimicked their Western neighbours' business activity tax rates, but this phenomenon manifested solely in the first years after reunification, later disappearing.

Among others, research on the supra-municipality level was conducted by L. P. Feld and E. Reulier (2005). The authors focused on the tax policy pursued by Swiss cantons from 1984 to 1999, and their results confirmed the existence of strategic tax competition about income tax. The relatively intense tax competition concerning personal income tax on the level of cantons and municipalities was also suggested in earlier research by L. P. Feld and G. Kirchgässner (2001). S. Rossi and B. Dafflon (2004) examined tax competition in the context of achieving lasting competitive advantages in a closed economy. The authors studied this phenomenon in the example of Swiss cantons in 1985–2001, noting, among others, that tax incentives meant to attract enterprises to a particular location will not be effective since tax competition mechanisms operate to eliminate all competitive advantages in the longer term. In addition, due to budget limitations, lowering the tax charges of entrepreneurs can force some of these charges to shift to other factors or activities.

Local tax competition has also elicited interest among researchers from other European countries, such as Finland. Since the decisive majority of tax revenue of Finnish municipalities is derived from income tax, the study of A. Kangasharju, A. Moisio, E. Reulier, and Y. Rocaboy (2006), covering the years 1988–2002, focuses on the rates of this tax. The presence of strategic interactions in establishing the rates of this tax was confirmed, and the scale of interactions was comparable to that observed in other studies. This was especially interesting since expectations assumed that the Scandinavian model of strongly equalised revenue would tend to restrict the tax competition phenomenon. On the other hand, studies conducted by T. Lyytikäinen (2012) did not confirm the presence of real estate tax competition between neighbouring Finnish municipalities.

The local tax competition phenomenon was less frequently subjected to empirical analyses by Central and Eastern European researchers. One of a few such studies was produced by L. Sedmihradská and E. Bakoš (2016), who examined using the so-called local coefficient in determining real estate tax rates. The research employing a binary logit model confirmed the presence of tax competition regardless of the kind of municipalities analysed and the neighbourhood definition used.

In Poland, an extensive study of tax competition on the local level was conducted by P. Swianiewicz and J. Łukomska (2016) based on data from the Rb-27 budget reports and supplemented by interviews conducted in 36 municipalities in 2014. An assumption was made for modelling that municipalities compete mainly with units in their immediate neighbourhood. The authors focused on the real estate tax (with taxes levied on natural and legal persons analysed separately), agricultural tax, and transport vehicles tax, covering units from the Dolnośląskie, Lubelskie, and Zachodniopomorskie provinces (about 500 municipalities in total). The study's primary purpose was to answer whether tax competition could be observed on the local level.

The results demonstrated that municipalities consider the rates in neighbouring areas when developing their own tax policy, which was confirmed by analysing correlation coefficients for rates used by each municipality and its neighbours. The authors also examined whether a change of rates triggers similar activities in adjacent municipalities, but such relationships were observed infrequently and not for all the taxes. Correlation and regression analyses were also used in subsequent stages of the study. The dependence between the number of tax rates and the diversity of rates in neighbouring municipalities was weak. A stronger relationship was visible in the case of taxes with a less mobile tax base, suggesting that yardstick competition rather than tax-based competition could occur. The correlation analysis showed that tax competition processes are more likely in regions with higher levels of bridging social capital, with greater importance of comparative competition in contrast to tax base competition. In addition, the results suggested that tax competition might occur more often in smaller municipalities, especially those near large cities.

To summarise, it is worth citing a few conclusions from a study by H. Blöchliger and J. Pinero-Campos (2011), formulated based on the results of tax competition research conducted in OECD countries. They noticed that tax policy interactions are ubiquitous in most countries concerning all taxes and levels of public authority. Local authorities treat tax policy as a means to extend the mobile tax base, even though political motives are also often necessary. Some taxes (income taxes) are more susceptible to the tax competition phenomenon, while others (real estate taxes) are much less. In the case of consumption taxes, the size of the unit is of significant importance. In some studies, a tendency to converge tax rates was visible, and tax competition often increased rather than lowered tax rates. It was also observed that high enforceability of taxes correlated with low tax rates, while broader tax autonomy led to less disproportionate taxes. These conclusions and the research results outlined above show that the local tax competition phenomenon cannot be unequivocally evaluated, which remains an exciting area of academic exploration.

1.4.2 The PBC in local governments

As the PBC theory developed, researchers increasingly began to ask themselves: Is the cycle also visible on the local, supralocal, or regional level? This is not surprising since, in the 1990s, many countries saw the decentralisation of public finance systems reach its climax (Boex and Simatupang 2008; Manor 2006), prompting questions about the possibility of politicians influencing the results of local elections.

As mentioned earlier, analysis of the PBC on the level of local governments is much easier than on the nationwide level due to the limited scope of instruments (and consequently directions of influence) that local authorities can use. At the same time, researchers can usually take advantage of a large set of empirically verifiable data and local government regulations that are unified nationally (for example, regarding financial management), allowing comparison between units (Babczuk 2009).

Empirical research, verifying whether the PBC can occur at the level of local government authorities, has been conducted since the 1990s (Mouritzen 1989; Mouriuen 1989; Rosenberg 1992). Due to the complex and interdisciplinary nature of the issue, the conducted research focused on various aspects related to the appearance of the PBC. From the viewpoint of the financial management of local governments, it should be noted that the undertaken research deals with areas such as:

- expenditure policy, including the influence of fiscal rules (Bonfatti and Forni 2019; Bee and Moulton 2015; da Fonseca 2020; Olejnik 2019b);

- yardstick competition (Ferraresi 2020; Klien 2015);
- influencing tax revenues, including imposing taxes and establishing fees or penalties;
- the issue of balance and deficit (Ehrhart 2013; Mouriuen 1989; Babczuk 2009);
- influence (pressure) of the media on politicians;
- the impact of voter preferences on decisions of authorities;
- the impact of government transfers on the PBC, including the "indirect PBC" theory,
- the impact of social capital on PBC (Batinti, Andriani, and Filippetti 2019);
- correctness of local tax revenue projections;
- visibility or salience of instruments;
- the political orientation of parties (Bastida, Estrada, and Guillamón 2021).

F. Bastida, L. Estrada, and M.-D. Gullamón (2021) analysed relationships between the political orientation of the ruling party (right- or left-wing) and the level of expenditure for 299 local government units in Honduras. Their research results point to a partisan PBC in some local governments since parties with left-wing views note an increase in total expenditures around the election date.

In 2019–2021, M. Ferraresi published a series of articles devoted to the PBC. Together with Galmarini, Rizzo, and Zanardi (2019), he analysed the impact of the expected replacement of the leading residential real estate tax on the political cycle for more than 700 Italian municipalities in 2002–2008 (elections) and in 2007–2009 (financial figures). The study concluded that the PBC occurring in Italian municipalities was enhanced by an external factor, namely information about the partial abolition of the real estate tax and its replacement with transfers from the state budget, which led to lower revenue. The study suggested that in the municipalities where elections took place, one year after the reform, they increased their expenditures by 3% and revenue from fees and commissions by 10% compared to the average value in the pre-election (reform) year. The increase in revenue from fees and commissions was the result of local governments "unburdening" taxpayers of the real estate tax (a significant decrease in tax charges) and taking advantage of voters being "accustomed" to the existence of tax charges (increased fees and commissions). As a result, increased fees formed the basis for financing an increase in expenditure (which was dictated by the intention of the incumbents to be re-elected). No such dependencies were observed in local governments in which elections preceded reforms. M. Ferraresi also conducted a similar study concerning tax revenue (in this case, from real estate tax). However, the results did not demonstrate the presence of yardstick competition. In another article (Ferraresi 2020), he expanded upon his previous research on the political cycle, noting the presence of *yardstick competition* between municipalities in which power is wielded by coalitions having a slight majority and by mayors who seek re-election. The research covered 2001–2011 and some 75% of Italian municipalities. Ferraresi took advantage of the temporal shift in electoral cycles in individual municipalities. The most recent of his published articles (Ferraresi 2021), on the other hand, is a multi-dimensional analysis of data on tax rates (including real estate tax rates) and fees in Italian municipalities, which refers, on the one hand, to tax competition between municipalities (*spatial correlation*) and, on the other, to the "visibility" and "salience" of tax. Regarding visible and salient fees and taxes, the authorities greatly lower the rates before the election. In contrast, the rates are increased for less transparent and salient taxes (for example, the extra local government component of personal income tax).

G. E. Wiguna and K. Khoirunurrofik (2021) analysed the amount of the budget (total revenue, expenditure, and deficit), components of own revenue (including the regional tax), and categories of expenditure (nine main directions and three main kinds of expenditure – goods and services, capital, and employment) for 499 regional governments in Indonesia, with the research covering the years 2011–2017. PBCs were identified for all components of own revenues (dropping in the election year) and expenditures relevant to improving residents' quality of life (rising in the election year). Analysing the total figures of revenue and spending showed their increase in the election year, a fact that, according to the authors, demonstrates the use of debt instruments as a source of financing and confirms the existence of the PBC.

On the other hand, G. Crispim, L. Alberton, C. D. Ferreira, and J. E. de Gusmão Lopes (2020) analysed changes in the financial management of local governments of large Brazilian cities, taking into account, among others, the structure of revenue and expenditure. The hypotheses they proposed were related to the impact of the PBC on total spending and investment expenditure, the level of loan streams, and compliance with fiscal regulations. While the research results did not confirm the assumption that total expenditure is growing, a 9% increase in investment expenditure and a 68% increase in loans were noted compared to non-election years. In addition, the research showed that election years witness more instances in which public finance regulations on fund management (financing electoral campaigns) are violated.

Other factors affecting the amount of expenditure in the PBC were noted by L. Repetto (2018), who began to analyse the impact that the availability of information about financial management and activities of local governments in Italy had on the level of manipulating budget expenditures in the pre-election period. He noted essential differences between local governments in which the availability of such information was lower (a greater tendency to manipulate and more significant increases in expenditure) and governments in which citizens were duly informed about government activities.

Research undertaken by a team led by B. Cuadrado-Ballesteros and I. M. Garcia-Sanchez (2018) dealt with the propensity of the ruling circles (in this case, 145 Spanish municipalities from 2005 to 2013) to engage in opportunistic or partisan behaviours that trigger a PBC given different levels of pressure from the media and various levels of fragmentation of the political scene. The research results make it plain that citizens' access to information is vital since the tendency to manipulate (including taxes) is more significant when media pressure and the availability of information are low.

The research by A. Corvalan, P. Cox, and R. Osorio (2018) yielded significant findings. Their analysis of an indirect political budget cycle, defined as PBC, triggered by government transfers to local governments, where the ruling clique belonged to the same party as the central authorities, is particularly noteworthy. The study, which focused on Chilean local governments, revealed that government transfers played a crucial role in supporting the PBC by causing a surge in the expenditure of selected local governments around the election date. This effect was particularly pronounced in local government units at risk of being won back by the opposition.

A. Alesina and M. Paradisi (2017) analysed the tendency of Italian local governments to lower real estate tax rates after the former real estate tax (ICI) was replaced by a new tax (IMU) in 2011. In the new scheme, local governments were granted much more discretion in setting tax rates, and the rule that taxation applies to the principal place of residence was reinstated. Research results demonstrated that smaller local governments, in particular, tended to lower these rates in 2012, if 2013 was their election year. Manipulating the rates in these municipalities, in the authors' opinion, caused the deficit per capita to increase by 6% in the election year. The authors stress that citizens' negative attitude towards the real estate tax is the main factor affecting the authorities' decisions. Lowering the tax rates could, therefore, serve as a powerful bargaining chip that influences the results of elections.

S. Garmann (2017) conducted a study on the influence of citizen attitudes towards fiscal policy on the tendency of local authorities in Hessian municipalities to manipulate public expenditures. The study, which used the "fiscal conservatism" level as a benchmark, measured according to the referenda results on introducing a "fiscal brake" to limit the number of budget deficits, highlighted the significant role of fiscal conservatism. The research results show that the fiscal conservatism of voters in studied local governments may translate into decisions of those in power to increase expenditure in the pre-election period. S. Garmann notes that voters tended to display low conservatism in local governments, increasing expenditure (consent). In contrast, expenditure dipped firmly in pre-election periods in governments with high estimated conservatism. According to S. Garmann, this reflected the manipulations undertaken by those in power motivated by the beliefs of the majority of voters.

The research by T. Baskaran, A. Brender, S. Blesse, and Y. Reingewertz (2016) addressed a crucial question: Do the decentralisation of expenditures and the financial oversight of the government influence the occurrence of PBCs and their intensity? Their analysis of budget, socio-economic, and political data of 1,212 Israeli municipalities from 1999 to 2009, without breaking it down by detailed sources of revenue, provided important insights. The team's analysis showed that a high dependence on government transfers, reflected in the low share of locally obtained revenues in the municipality budget, makes PBCs more intense. In contrast, they disappear when a close monitoring approach is followed, under which the central government appoints external accountants in municipalities that run into debt. The main direction of increasing expenditure in pre-election periods was pro-development objectives since, as the authors argue, conscious voters saw such expenditures as the only justified reason for increasing local government deficits.

In turn, C. A. Bee and S. R. Moulton (2015) analysed the revenue, expenditures, budget balances, and employment levels in the local governments of 268 US cities from 1970 to 2004. Their hypothesis about opportunistic PBCs in the studied local governments was confirmed only concerning increasing employment in the local government sector (police, administration, and education).

M. E. Binet and J. S. Pentecote (2004) analysed the revenue and expenditure of 883 French municipalities from 1988 to 1999 (1989 and 1995 were election years). Their research shows that an opportunistic PBC exists, manifesting in a periodic decrease in revenue from local taxes (including real estate taxes).

L. Sedmihradská (2013) proposed another view of PBC, focusing on analysing the scale of underestimating the projected revenue of 198 Czech municipalities in 2003–2011 in the context of the PBC. According to her, during the studied period, the municipalities tended to lower planned revenue, while in election years, the projected revenue from local taxes was considerably more accurate (Sedmihradska 2013, 291–292).

M. Lopes da Fonseca (2020) analysed the fiscal policy of 150 mayors of Portuguese local governments who, due to the limitation in the number of terms introduced in 2006, could not be elected again in the 2013 elections (*lame ducks*). On the revenue side, she focused on the real estate tax, which the mayors lowered during their last term. In contrast, on the expenditure side, she considered total expenditure and expenditure related to employment in local government institutions. This expenditure was also found to have decreased, contradicting the results obtained by a team led by J. Alt (2011), which demonstrated a rise in tax rates for soon-to-be out-of-office incumbents.

M. U. Gutierrez (2021) analysed the main factors affecting the revenue from real estate tax in Mexican urban municipalities from 1990 to 2010. The results of his research suggest that municipal tax policies vary depending on the degree of political rivalry. As the opposition parties grow in power, the tendency to increase real estate tax rates diminishes. At the same time, his results did not demonstrate any impact of government transfers on municipal tax policy (in contrast to the results published by other authors).

A. Batinti and his associates (2019) assessed the influence of social capital on the direction of expenditures and the level of taxes (real estate and the extra local PIT component) in Italian municipalities between 2003 and 2012. The study was concluded by demonstrating that as the social capital of a municipality's inhabitants grows, there is a change in their preferences as to the directions of expenditure (more substantial interest in long-term development expenditure) and sources of revenue (increasing acceptance of the real estate tax), impacting the decisions the mayors have to make to secure re-election.

M. Klien (2014) focused his studies on how the base fee for water supply developed in 74 Austrian local governments from 1993 to 2009. As a result, he demonstrated that fee increases in pre-election periods are decisively less frequent and smaller than at other times. In his opinion, municipality authorities hold back increases in the pre-election period, and even if they do not, the increases are usually aligned with inflation, which the voters see as a rational justification. M. Klein asserts that leaving rates unchanged is also a feature of the PBC. In another 2015 article, he dealt with *yardstick competition* as a component of the PBC (Klien 2015).

B. Benito, M. D. Guillamón, and A. M. Rios published two articles (2021a, 2021b) on the discretionary application of penalties by Spanish local government authorities in the pre-election period. Their research demonstrated unequivocally that the possibility of affecting the level of such revenues for election-related purposes exists since the amount of such revenue is lower in the pre-election period than in other years.

On the other hand, L. G. Veiga and F. J. Veiga (2007) showcased research results on the PBC in Portuguese municipalities. The data analysis demonstrates that in the pre-election period, the behaviour of municipality authorities was opportunistic (motivated by their wish for re-election), which led to increasing expenditure before the elections and changing their structure to be more visible and salient for voters. Tax rates, which the municipal authorities are competent to set, were also lowered. However, the data were presented for aggregated values of taxes.

H. Ehrhart (2013) and P. E. Mouritzen (1989), independently of each other, tackled the issue of analysing general data about fiscal policies of local governments in several countries and also demonstrated the variation in occurrences of the PBC and instruments used by specific governments.

In Poland, researchers take up the issue of PBC with local government authorities relatively infrequently. One of the first authors who referred to the PBC in Polish local governments was A. Babczuk (2009), who researched the variability of the budget deficit level in Polish municipalities as a result of occurrences of the PBC. Based on research carried out for most municipalities in Poland from 1992 to 2008, he pointed out that about 30% of them noted more profound deficits around the election date, which confirms that the PBC does occur in these municipalities.

S. Bartnicki (2018), similar to P. Kukołowicz and M. Górecki (2018), analysed how investments influence voter attitudes according to the opportunistic

PBC theory. He demonstrated that property investment expenditures in the election year and earlier significantly impact voters. Another area of manipulation, which he noticed using the results of his research, was increasing expenditures on wages.

A team consisting of A. Malkowska, M. Głuszak, B. Marona, and A. Telega (2020) tackled the issue of the impact of the electoral cycle on the policy of local governments regarding real estate tax rates in ten Polish metropolitan areas (300 municipalities), with research covering the years 2005–2015. The conclusions of the analysis suggest that a relationship exists between the electoral cycle and the level of tax rates in the studied municipalities. According to the authors, lowering rates in the pre-election period is a symptom of the opportunistic behaviour of municipal authorities.

On the other hand, L. Olejnik, in his articles, took up the issue of using tickets and fines (among others) as a budget policy instrument related to the PBC. Research conducted on data from 2007 to 2017 for all Polish municipalities did not confirm a drop in revenue from those sources in pre-election years (Olejnik 2019a). In another article (Olejnik 2019b), he analysed the variability of expenditure on wages in county-level local governments from 2007 to 2018 and in province-level local governments from 1999 to 2018. Data analysis demonstrated that (opportunity) PBCs occur in the studied units and are reflected by significant increases in expenditure for wages before elections. This is the case, particularly for local governments where the dominant party has a solid coalition-building capability.

W. Bień undertook to analyse the relationship between the electoral cycle and tax policy in all 182 municipalities of the Małopolskie province from 2006 to 2018. Her research demonstrated that "the role of local taxes in building political capital before local elections is practically non-existent" (Bień 2021). The study did not analyse tax rate changes; instead, data from RB-PDP reports on gaps in tax revenues were used.

P. Swianiewicz and A. Kurniewicz (2018), together with D. Kalcheva (2019), tackled the issue of municipal services fees related to the supply of water and collection of sewage (whose specific character causes them to be classified as para-taxes or *earmarked taxes*), as well as fees for public housing and public transportation tickets. In their works, they noticed that even when the residents sustained such charges, the impact of the electoral cycle on how rates for such services evolved varied.

As can be seen, the PBC in local government authorities is a complex issue whose analysis may extend considerably beyond municipal tax policy.

Note

1 To this end, the municipality uses tax-related powers that consist of the ability to shape tax rates, introduce tax credits, and grant remittances and exemptions in real estate tax, agricultural tax, forest tax and transport vehicles tax.

Bibliography

Agrawal, David R. 2015. "The Tax Gradient: Spatial Aspects of Fiscal Competition." *American Economic Journal: Economic Policy* 7 (2): 1–29. doi:10.1257/pol.20120360.

Alesina, Alberto. 1987. "Macroeconomic Policy in a Two-Party System as a Repeated Game." *The Quarterly Journal of Economics* 102 (3): 651–678.

Alesina, Alberto, and Matteo Paradisi. 2017. "Political Budget Cycles: Evidence from Italian Cities." *Economics & Politics* 29 (2): 157–177. doi:10.1111/ecpo.12091.

Alesina, Alberto, Nouriel Roubini, and Gerald D. Cohen. 1997. *Political Cycles and the Macroeconomy*. Cambridge: MIT Press.

Alt, James, Ethan Bueno de Mesquita, and Shanna Rose. 2011. "Disentangling Accountability and Competence in Elections: Evidence from U.S. Term Limits." *The Journal of Politics* 73 (1): 171–186. doi:10.1017/s0022381610000940.

Babczuk, Arkadiusz. 2009. "Polityczny Cykl Budżetowy w Polskich Gminach." *Zeszyty Naukowe Uniwersytetu Szczecińskiego* 526: 44–50.

Bartnicki, Sławomir. 2018. "Wybrane fiskalne instrumenty walki o głosy w wyborach bezpośrednich gminnego organu wykonawczego w Polsce i uwarunkowania ich stosowania." *Studia Socjologiczno-Polityczne. Seria Nowa* 8 (1): 53–76.

Baskaran, Thushyanthan. 2020. "Fiscal Interactions in the Short and the Long Run: Evidence from German Reunification." *Journal of Economic Geography* 20 (3): 711–732. doi:10.1093/jeg/lby068.

Baskaran, Thushyanthan, Adi Brender, Sebastian Blesse, and Yaniv Reingewertz. 2016. "Revenue Decentralization, Central Oversight and the Political Budget Cycle: Evidence from Israel." *European Journal of Political Economy* 42 (March): 1–16. doi:10.1016/j.ejpoleco.2015.12.001.

Bastida, Francisco, Lorenzo Estrada, and María-Dolores Guillamón. 2021. "Flypaper Effect and Partisanship Theories Best Explain Municipal Financial Performance in Latin America." *Policy Studies* 0 (0): 1298–1321. doi:10.1080/01442872.2021.1982887.

Batinti, Alberto, Luca Andriani, and Andrea Filippetti. 2019. "Local Government Fiscal Policy, Social Capital and Electoral Payoff: Evidence across Italian Municipalities." *Kyklos* 72 (4): 503–526. doi:10.1111/kykl.12209.

Batorski, Dominik, and Wieslaw Bartkowski. 2003. "Identyfikacja Partyjna w Przestrzennej Teorii Wyborów." *Studia Socjologiczne* 1 (January): 113.

Bee, C. Adam, and Shawn R. Moulton. 2015. "Political Budget Cycles in U.S. Municipalities." *Economics of Governance* 16 (4): 379–403. doi:10.1007/s10101-015-0171-z.

Benito, Bernardino, María-Dolores Guillamón, and Anna-Maria Ríos. 2021a. "Political Budget Cycles in Public Revenues: Evidence from Fines." *Sage Open* 11 (4): 1–13. doi:10.1177/21582440211059169.

Benito, Bernardino, María-Dolores Guillamón, and Anna-Maria Ríos. 2021b. "Are Politicians Using Fines for Electoral Purposes? Empirical Evidence." *Revista Espanola de Financiacion y Contabilidad* 50 (3): 338–358. doi:10.1080/02102412.2020.1815966.

Besley, Timothy, and Anne Case. 1995. "Incumbent Behavior: Vote–Seeking, Tax–Setting, and Yardstick Competition." *American Economic Review* 85: 25–45.

Bickers, Kenneth N., and Robert M. Stein. 1996. "The Electoral Dynamics of the Federal Pork Barrel." *American Journal of Political Science* 40 (4): 1300–1326. doi:10.2307/2111752.

Bień, Wioletta. 2021. "The Electoral Cycle and the Tax Policy of Gminas." *Studia Prawno-Ekonomiczne* 118 (May): 139–158. doi:10.26485/SPE/2021/118/8.

Binet, Marie-Estelle, and Jean-Sébastien Pentecôte. 2004. "Tax Degression and the Political Budget Cycle in French Municipalities." *Applied Economics Letters* 11 (14): 905–908. doi:10.1080/1350485042000268642.

Black, Duncan. 1948. "On the Rationale of Group Decision-Making." *Journal of Political Economy* 56 (1): 23–34. doi:10.1086/256633.

Blöchliger, Hansjörg, ed. 2013. *Fiscal Federalism 2014: Making Decentralisation Work*. Paris: OECD. https://dx. doi.org/10.1787/9789264204577-en.

Blöchliger, Hansjörg, and José Maria Pinero-Campos. 2011. *Tax Competition between Sub-Central Governments* 13 (2011): 1–48. doi:10.1787/5kgb1mfm6jnw-en.

Boex, Jameson, and Renata R. Simatupang. 2008. "Fiscal Decentralisation and Empowerment: Evolving Concepts and Alternative Measures." *Fiscal Studies* 29 (4): 435–465.

Bonfatti, Andrea, and Lorenzo Forni. 2019. "Fiscal Rules to Tame the Political Budget Cycle: Evidence from Italian Municipalities." *European Journal of Political Economy* 60 (December): 101800. doi:10.1016/j.ejpoleco.2019.06.001.

Brett, Craig, and Joris Pinkse. 2000. "The Determinants of Municipal Tax Rates in British Columbia." *Canadian Journal of Economics* 33 (3): 695–714. doi:10.1111/0008-4085.00037.

Buchanan, James M. 1960. "The Theory of Public Finance." edited by Richard A. Musgrave. *Southern Economic Journal* 26 (3): 234–238. doi:10.2307/1054956.

Case, Anne. 1993. "Interstate Tax Competition After TRA86." *Journal of Policy Analysis and Management* 12: 136–148.

Corvalan, Alejandro, Paulo Cox, and Rodrigo Osorio. 2018. "Indirect Political Budget Cycles: Evidence from Chilean Municipalities." *Journal of Development Economics* 133 (July): 1–14. doi:10.1016/j.jdeveco.2018.01.001.

Crispim, Gilberto, Luiz Alberton, Celma Duque Ferreira, and Jorge Expedito de Gusmao Lopes. 2020. "Behavior of Budget Expenditures During the Election Period: An Analysis in Panel Data in the Brazilian Municipalities." *Revista Ambiente Contabil* 12 (2): 179–199. doi:10.21680/2176-9036.2020v12n2ID19072.

Cuadrado-Ballesteros, Beatriz, and Isabel-Maria Garcia-Sanchez. 2018. "Conditional Factors of Political Budget Cycles: Economic Development Media Pressure, and Political Fragmentation." *Public Performance & Management Review* 41 (4): 835–858. doi:10.1080/15309576.2018.1465829.

Cunow, S., Desposato, S., Janusz, A., & Sells, C. (2021). "Less is more: The paradox of choice in voting behavior." *Electoral Studies* 69: 102230.

da Fonseca, Mariana Lopes. 2020. "Lame Ducks and Local Fiscal Policy: Quasi-Experimental Evidence from Portugal." *Economic Journal* 130 (626). Oxford: Oxford University Press: 511–533. doi:10.1093/ej/uez042.

Dafflon, Bernard. 2014. "Panorama des impôts en Suisse. Du local au fédéral, entre équité et concurrence: quels enjeux?" *Domaine Public*. https://www.domainepublic.ch/docs/2014/DP_2058_2014_11_14.pdf.

Downs, Anthony. 1957. *An Economic Theory of Democracy*. New York: HarperCollins Publishers.

Drazen, Allan, and Marcela Eslava. 2006. *Pork Barrel Cycles*. Working Paper 12190. Working Paper Series. National Bureau of Economic Research. doi:10.3386/w12190.

Drazen, Allan, and Marcela Eslava. 2010. "Electoral Manipulation via Voter-Friendly Spending: Theory and Evidence." *Journal of Development Economics* 92 (1): 39–52. doi:10.1016/j.jdeveco.2009.01.001.

Ehrhart, Helene. 2013. "Elections and the Structure of Taxation in Developing Countries." *Public Choice* 156 (1): 195–211. doi:10.1007/s11127-011-9894-8.

Enkelmann, S., and M. Leibrecht. 2013. "Political Expenditure Cycles and Election Outcomes: Evidence from Disaggregation of Public Expenditures by Economic Functions." *Economics Letters* 121 (1): 128–132. doi:10.1016/j.econlet.2013.07.015.

Eslava, Marcela. 2005. *Political Budget Cycles or Voters as Fiscal Conservatives? Evidence From Colombia*. 003343. *Documentos CEDE*. Documentos CEDE. Universidad de los Andes - CEDE. https://ideas.repec.org/p/col/000089/003343.html.

Europejska Karta Samorządu Terytorialnego (Lokalnego) Sporządzona w Strasburgu Dnia 15 Października 1985r. 1994. *Dz.U. 1994 Nr 124 Poz. 607 Oraz Dz.U. 2006 Nr 154 Poz. 1107.*

Famulska, Teresa, Ryta Dziemianowicz, Krzysztof Biernacki, and Beata Rogowska-Rajda. 2019. *Wydajność fiskalna podatkowych źródeł dochodów jednostek samorządu terytorialnego w Polsce*. Wrocław: Wydawnictwo Uniwersytetu Ekonomicznego.

Feld, Lars P., and Gebhard Kirchgässner. 2001. "Income Tax Competition at the State and Local Level in Switzerland." *Regional Science and Urban Economics* 31 (2–3): 181–213.

Feld, Lars P., and Emmanuelle Reulier. 2005. "Strategic Tax Competition in Switzerland: Evidence from a Panel of The Swiss Cantons." *CESifo Working Paper* no. 1516.

Felis, Paweł, and Grzegorz Otczyk. 2021. "Zróżnicowanie fiskalnych skutków gminnej polityki podatkowej w Polsce." *Studia BAS* 1 (65). doi:10.31268/StudiaBAS.2021.06.

Felis, Paweł, Elżbieta Malinowska-Misiąg, Grzegorz Otczyk, and Henryk Rosłaniec, eds. 2020. *Planowanie Dochodów z Podatków Lokalnych w Polsce*. Wydanie I. Warszawa: Oficyna Wydawnicza SGH.

Ferraresi, Massimiliano. 2020. "Political Cycles, Spatial Interactions and Yardstick Competition: Evidence from Italian Cities." *Journal of Economic Geography* 20 (4): 1093–1115. doi:10.1093/jeg/lbz036.

Ferraresi, Massimiliano. 2021. "Political Budget Cycle, Tax Collection, and Yardstick Competition." *The B.E. Journal of Economic Analysis & Policy*. doi:10.1515/bejeap-2020-0380.

Garmann, Sebastian. 2017. "Political Budget Cycles and Fiscally Conservative Voters." *Economics Letters* 155 (June): 72–75. doi:10.1016/j.econlet.2017.03.023.

Gentry, M., N. Greenhalgh-Stanley, S.M. Rohlin, and J.P. Thompson. 2020. "Dynamic Sales Tax Competition: Evidence from Panel Data at the Border, 'Working Papers.'" Boston, MA: Federal Reserve Bank of Boston. doi:10.29412/res.wp.2020.05.

Gutierrez, Monica Unda. 2021. "Poor Local Finances: What Explains Property Tax Collection in Mexico?" *Estudios Demograficos Y Urbanos* 36 (1): 49–88. doi:10.24201/edu.v36i1.1871.

Hauptmeier, Sebastian, Ferdinand Mittermaier, and Johannes Rincke. 2009. "Fiscal Competition over Taxes and Public Inputs Theory and Evidence." *EBC Working Paper Series* 1033 (March).

Hendrick, R., Y. Wu, and B. Jacob. 2007. "Tax Competition Among Municipal Governments: Exit Versus Voice." *Urban Affairs Review* 43 (2): 221–255. doi:10.1177/1078087407305312.

Heyndels, Bruno, and Jef Vuchelen. 1998. "Tax Mimicking among Belgian Municipalities." *National Tax Journal* 51 (1): 89–101.

Hibbs, Douglas A. 1977. "Political Parties and Macroeconomic Policy*." *American Political Science Review* 71 (4): 1467–1487. doi:10.1017/S0003055400269712.

Hoare, A. G. 1983. "Pork-Barrelling in Britain: A Review." *Environment and Planning C: Government and Policy* 1 (4): 413–438. doi:10.1068/c010413.

Janeba, Eckhard, and Steffen Osterloh. 2013. "Tax and the City: A Theory of Local Tax Competition and Evidence for Germany." *ZEW Discussion Papers*, no. 12-005[rev.].

Jayet, Hubert, and Sonia Paty. 2006. "Capital Indivisibility and Tax Competition: Are There Too Many Business Areas When Some of Them Are Empty?" *Journal of Urban Economics* 60 (3): 399–417. doi:10.1016/j.jue.2006.04.001.

Kalecki, M. 1943. "Political Aspects of Full Employment1." *The Political Quarterly* 14 (4): 322–330. doi:10.1111/j.1467-923X.1943.tb01016.x.

Kangasharju, Aki, Antti Moisio, Emmanuelle Reulier, and Yvon Rocaboy. 2006. "Tax competition among municipalities in Finland." *Urban Public Economics Review* 5: 12–23.

Khemani, Stuti. 2000. *Political Cycles in a Developing Economy: Effect of Elections in Indian States*. Washington, DC: World Bank. doi:10.1596/1813-9450-2454.

Klien, Michael. 2014. "Tariff Increases over the Electoral Cycle: A Question of Size and Salience." *European Journal of Political Economy* 36 (December): 228–242. doi:10.1016/j.ejpoleco.2014.08.004.

Klien, Michael. 2015. "The Political Side of Public Utilities: How Opportunistic Behaviour and Yardstick Competition Shape Water Prices in Austria." *Papers in Regional Science* 94 (4). doi:10.1111/pirs.12101.

Konstytucja Rzeczypospolitej Polskiej. 1997. https://isap.sejm.gov.pl/isap.nsf/DocDetails.xsp?id=WDU19970780483.

Kukołowicz, Paula, and Maciej A. Górecki. 2018. "When Incumbents Can Only Gain: Economic Voting in Local Government Elections in Poland." *West European Politics* 41 (3): 640–659. doi:10.1080/01402382.2017.1403147.

Ladd, Helen. 1992. "Mimicking of Local-Tax Burdens Among Neighboring Counties." *Public Finance Quarterly* 20 (4): 450–467. doi:10.1177/109114219202000404.

Le Maux, Benoit. 2007. "Is the Median Voter Really Decisive? Evidence from French Municipalities." *Revue D Economie Regionale Et Urbaine* 5 (December): 921–944. doi:10.3917/reru.075.0921.

Łukomska, Julita, and Paweł Swianiewicz. 2015. *Polityka Podatkowa Władz Lokalnych w Polsce*. Warszawa: Municipium SA.

Lyytikäinen, Teemu. 2012. "Tax Competition among Local Governments: Evidence from a Property Tax Reform in Finland." *Journal of Public Economics* 96 (7): 584–595. doi:10.1016/j.jpubeco.2012.03.002.

Malkowska, Agnieszka, Michal Gluszak, Bartlomiej Marona, and Agnieszka Telega. 2020. "The Impact of the Electoral Cycle on Area-Based Property Tax in Poland." *Eastern European Economics* 58 (6): 517–535. doi:10.1080/00128775.2020.1798160.

Manor, James. 2006. "Renewing the Debate on Decentralisation." *Commonwealth & Comparative Politics* 44 (3): 283–288. doi:10.1080/14662040600996967.

Mintz, Jack, and Michael Smart. 2004. "Income Shifting, Investment, and Tax Competition: Theory and Evidence from Provincial Taxation in Canada." *Journal of Public Economics* 88 (ue 6): 1149–1168. doi:10.1016/S0047-2727(03)00060-4.

Mouritzen, Poul Erik. 1989. "City Size and Citizens' Satisfaction: Two Competing Theories Revisited." *European Journal of Political Research* 17 (6): 661–688.

Mouriuen, Poul Erik. 1989. "The Local Political Business Cycle." *Scandinavian Political Studies* 12 (1): 37–55.

Müller, Wolfgang C., and Kaare Strøm, eds. 1999. *Policy, Office, or Votes?: How Political Parties in Western Europe Make Hard Decisions*. Cambridge Studies in Comparative Politics. Cambridge: Cambridge University Press. doi:10.1017/CBO9780511625695.

Musgrave, Richard A. 1959. *The Theory of Public Finance: A Study in Public Economy*. New York: McGraw-Hill.

Nordhaus, William D. 1975. "The Political Business Cycle." *Review of Economic Studies* 42 (2). Oxford University Press: 169–190.

Nordhaus, William D. 1989. "Alternative Approaches to the Political Business Cycle." *Brookings Papers on Economic Activity* 2: 1–69.

Oates, Wallace E. 1972. *Fiscal Federalism*. New York: Harcourt Brace Jovanovich.

Oates, Wallace E., and Robert M. Schwab. 1988. "Economic Competition among Jurisdictions: Efficiency Enhancing or Distortion Inducing?" *Journal of Public Economics* 35 (3): 333–354. doi:10.1016/0047-2727(88)90036-9.

Olejnik, Łukasz Wiktor. 2019a. "Mandaty i Grzywny w Polskich Gminach–Narzędzie Polityki Karnej Czy Polityki Budżetowej?" *Ruch Prawniczy, Ekonomiczny i Socjologiczny* 81 (3): 221–234.

Olejnik, Łukasz Wiktor. 2019b. "Local Political Business Cycles and Administration Spending in Polish Local Governments." *Economic and Regional Studies/Studia Ekonomiczne i Regionalne* 12 (2): 187–199. doi:10.2478/ers-2019-0017.

Oręziak, Leokadia. 2007. *Konkurencja Podatkowa i Harmonizacja Podatków w Ramach Unii Europejskiej: Implikacje Dla Polski*. Warszawa: Oficyna Wydawnicza Wyższej Szkoły Handlu i Prawa im. Ryszarda Łazarskiego.

Osborne, Martin J., and Al Slivinski. 1996. "A Model of Political Competition with Citizen-Candidates." *The Quarterly Journal of Economics* 111 (1): 65–96. doi:10.2307/2946658.

Patrzałek, Leszek. 1994. "Cele Polityki Podatkowej Gminy." *Samorząd Terytorialny* 12: 47–51.

Persson, Torsten, and Guido Tabellini. 1990. *Macroeconomic Policy, Credibility and Politics*. London: Routledge. https://www.routledge.com/Macroeconomic-Policy-Credibility-and-Politics/Persson-Tabellini/p/book/9780415510967.

Persson, Torsten, and Guido Tabellini. 2002. *Political Economics: Explaining Economic Policy*. Cambridge, MA: MIT Press.

Piotrowska-Marczak, Krystyna, ed. 2009. *Federalizm fiskalny w teorii i praktyce*. Warszawa: Difin.

Piwowarski, Radosław. 2014. "Strategie wyborcze w świetle wybranych teoretycznych modeli głosowania." *Studia Prawno-Ekonomiczne* 93: 275–287.

Poniatowicz, Marzanna. 2015. "Determinanty autonomii dochodowej samorządu terytorialnego w Polsce." *Nauki o Finansach* 1 (22): 11–30.

Poniatowicz, Marzanna, and Dorota Wyszkowska. 2014. "Stymulowanie rozwoju lokalnej przedsiębiorczości a konkurencja podatkowa gmin." *Zeszyty Naukowe Wyższej Szkoły Bankowej w Poznaniu* 52 nr 1 Finansowe i podatkowe aspekty rozwoju przedsiębiorczości w regionach: 73–93.

Przybysz, Dariusz. 2003. "Wyrazistość Kandydata Na Scenie Politycznej i Niepewność Wyborcy." *Studia Socjologiczne* 1 (168): 79–111.

Repetto, Luca. 2018. "Political Budget Cycles with Informed Voters: Evidence from Italy." *Economic Journal* 128 (616): 3320–3353. doi:10.1111/ecoj.12570.

Richard, Jean-Francios, Henry Tulkens, and Magali Verdonck. 2005. "Tax Interaction Dynamics among Belgian Municipalities 1984-1997." *CORE Discussion Paper* 2005/48.

Rizzo, L. 2010. "Interaction between Federal Taxation and Horizontal Tax Competition: Theory and Evidence from Canada." *Public Choice* 144 (1/2): 368–387.

Rogoff, Kenneth. 1990. "Equilibrium Political Budget Cycles." *American Economic Review* 80: 21–36.

Rogoff, Kenneth, and Anne Sibert. 1988. "Elections and Macroeconomic Policy Cycles." *Review of Economic Studies* 55 (1): 1–16.

Rosenberg, Jacob. 1992. "Rationality and the Political Business Cycle: The Case of Local Government." *Public Choice* 73 (1): 71–81.

Rossi, Sergio, and Bernard Dafflon. 2004. "Tax Competition between Subnational Governments: Theoretical and Regional Policy Issues with Reference to Switzerland, w." In *Finanzpolitik in Der Kontroverse*, edited by Eckhard Hein, Arne Heise, and Achim Truger, 227–250. Margburg: Metropolis.

Sedmihradska, Lucie. 2013. "Accuracy of Tax Revenue Forecasts in Czech Municipalities." In *Proceedings of the 17th International Conference Current Trends in Public Sector Research,* edited by L. Furova and D. Spalkova, 287–294. Brno: Masarykova Univ. https://www.webofscience.com/wos/woscc/full-record/WOS:000335696100031.

Shi, Min, and Jakob Svensson. 2003. "Political Budget Cycles: A Review of Recent Developments." *Nordic Journal of Political Economy* 29: 67–76.

Shi, Min, and Jakob Svensson. 2006. "Political Budget Cycles: Do They Differ across Countries and Why?" *Journal of Public Economics* 90 (8): 1367–1389. doi:10.1016/j.jpubeco.2005.09.009.

Swianiewicz, Paweł. 1996. *Zróżnicowanie polityk finansowych władz lokalnych*. Transformacja Gospodarki 73. Warszawa: Instytut Badań nad Gospodarką Rynkową.

Swianiewicz, Paweł, and Anna Kurniewicz. 2018. "Cykl Polityczny w Opłatach Za Lokalne Usługi Publiczne w Polsce." *Kwartalnik Naukowy. Studia Regionalne i Lokalne* 2/2018. doi:10.7366/1509499527204.

Swianiewicz, Paweł, and Julita Łukomska. 2016. "Lokalna konkurencja podatkowa w Polsce." *Studia Regionalne i Lokalne* 2 (64): 5–29. doi:10.7366/1509499526401.

Swianiewicz, Paweł, Anna Kurniewicz, and Desislava Kalcheva. 2019. "The Political Budget Cycle in Earmarked Taxes for Local Public Services: A Comparison of Poland and Bulgaria." *Journal of Comparative Policy Analysis: Research and Practice* 21 (5): 463–480. doi:10.1080/13876988.2019.1594775.

Tiebout, Charles M. 1956. "A Pure Theory of Local Expenditures." *Journal of Political Economy* 64 (5): 416–424.

Van Parys, Stefan, and Tom Verbeke. 2006. "Tax Competition among Belgian Municipalities: A Multidimensional Battle?" *Regional and Urban Modeling 283600100, EcoMod*: 1–23.

Veiga, Linda Gonçalves, and Francisco José Veiga. 2007. "Political Business Cycles at the Municipal Level." *Public Choice* 131 (1): 45–64. doi:10.1007/s11127-006-9104-2.

Walasik, Artur. 2014. "Zakres i metody konkurencji podatkowej między władzami lokalnymi." *Studia Ekonomiczne* 198 cz 1: 200–210.

Wiguna, Ghany Ellantia, and Khoirunurrofik Khoirunurrofik. 2021. "Political Budget Cycle Patterns and the Role of Coalition Parties in Shaping Indonesian Local Government Spending." *Asia-Pacific Journal of Regional Science* 5 (1): 41–64. doi:10.1007/s41685-020-00186-0.

Wilson, John Douglas. 1999. "Theories of Tax Competition." *National Tax Journal* 52 (2): 269–304. doi:10.1086/NTJ41789394.

2 Property tax as a local tax policy instrument

2.1 The role of local taxes in view of theoretical achievements

The literature indicates that there is no commonly accepted definition of local taxes. It varies from one country to another (Korolewska 2021). For instance, in the Polish literature, there are a few different approaches (Kornberger-Sokołowska 2001):

- a broad perspective, including all the taxes within the revenue of local government budgets;
- a narrower perspective, including only those taxes with at least some components of taxing power;
- the narrowest perspective, including only those taxes defined by the legislator as local taxes, i.e. those regulated by the law on local taxes and levies.

Considering the broadest perspective (related to the tax beneficiary, i.e. the tax-based budget), it may be said that all types of tax revenues that feed local government budgets are local taxes. In Poland, they are as follows: property tax, agricultural tax, forestry tax, tax on means of transport, tax on inheritance and donation, and tax on civil law transactions and local government shares in state taxes (PIT and CIT). In the case of the narrowest definition, they are only property taxes and taxes on means of transport, as in the legislature, the term "local taxes" is limited to these two only.

It seems that the most realistic approach is the one that considers the scope of taxing power delegated to local government units. In theory, the division of taxing power between the state and local government is regarded as a cornerstone setting the boundaries of the local government's financial autonomy. Taxing power consists of several elements, including the right to impose taxes, the right to design the content of the taxation technique (setting tax rates, granting tax preferences), the right to determine the principles of tax collection (tax collection, decisions on tax liability/arrears, modification of the content of tax liability, legal and tax sanctions). The relationship between

DOI: 10.4324/9781003530503-3

the scope of decentralisation and the scope of taxing power in local taxation, which varies significantly in the contemporary tax systems of individual countries, is not always close and direct. Adopting a more decentralised model does not necessarily automatically translate into more rights for local units. In Poland, the taxing power exercised by municipalities is considered defective (Wyszkowska 2017), yet it affects the generated revenue level. It includes the right of municipalities to diversify tax rates based on the object criterion, to apply for object exemptions, and to make use of remissions, instalments, and postponement of tax payment deadlines. The most important right is the one that deals with setting tax rates. Freedom in this respect is limited by the Constitution, which permits the resolution-making bodies only to reduce the maximum rates set out in the law of local taxes and levies and annually adjusted by the inflation index (in property tax and tax on means of transport) and to reduce an average purchase price of rye (in agricultural tax) or the sale price of wood (in forestry tax).

The difficulties in formulating a universal and precise definition of "local taxes" in science and based on tax legislation can be confirmed by the opinion of R. Bahl and R.M. Bird (2008), according to which entirely local taxes are levies in the case of local authorities have: the freedom to impose a tax; the right to establish the tax base; the right to set tax rates; the right to establish the tax assessment for each taxpayer in the case of direct taxation; the right to administer the tax; and the right to claim the entire revenue generated from the tax. Most local government taxes meet only a specific part of these conditions.

The outlined difficulties regarding formulating a uniform and precise definition of local taxes lead to the conclusion that we are indeed dealing with a set of taxes, conventionally called local taxes, determined exclusively by central authorities in most contemporary tax systems. It would, therefore, be necessary to devise a specific catalogue of characteristics according to which it would be possible to identify the taxes best fit to be called local taxes. A detailed approach was adopted by P. Swianiewicz, who listed (2004):

- efficiency adequate to the tasks performed (the tax base should create opportunities for local governments to obtain funds that would be comparable to those necessary to perform the tasks delegated to local governments);
- even spatial distribution of the tax base (being aware of the fact that few taxes can be entirely attributed to this feature, it is necessary to create a compensatory horizontal system);
- transparent territorial allocation (a clear-cut definition of the beneficiary of the revenue from a particular tax);
- a permanent spatial relationship of the tax base (the subject matter of a wealth tax is characterised by "location fixity", which prevents the source of the tax from moving to another place where the tax burden is lower, i.e. unhealthy tax competition);

- "tax visibility" (in other words, its "noticeability" is of particular importance precisely for local government units, and it favours the strengthening of local democracy);
- inflation-related flexibility (taxes that take into account inflation are more predictable so that local authorities have the freedom to plan their financial management);
- the principle of universality of the tax burden (the most significant possible proportion of taxpayers should bear the tax burden);
- simplicity and cheapness (the local tax system should be transparent, and the tax collection cost concerning tax efficiency should be low).

The above-mentioned tax principles are best met by the structures of property taxes (property tax) and income taxes (personal income tax). In European countries, the groups of local taxes are highly diverse, although models in which the most crucial local tax is a property tax or a local income tax are prevalent. Among the specific features indicated, those that are particularly important in the case of local taxes should be considered first. Of course, assuming local authorities have the appropriate power to adopt them.

Firstly, the universality of taxation. All taxes, including local ones, should be paid by the highest possible proportion of taxpayers. Placing the burden on the broadest possible group of local authority residents can increase the tax awareness of the inhabitants of a given region. By showing greater interest in local affairs, the residents of a municipality indirectly contribute to the development of local democracy (Karpus 2002).

Secondly, a sustainable spatial relationship of the tax base. Suppose the condition of the most robust possible confinement of taxes to the territory is met. In that case, transferring tax sources to places with a lower burden (disadvantageous for local governments) is avoided. By preventing tax competition, this feature generates systematic revenue necessary to finance the area's infrastructure to which certain taxes are permanently linked. It is evident that limiting the "migration of the tax base" is of great importance for the local government independently implementing the tax policy, and it is difficult to imagine a situation where undeveloped or developed property is transferred between different local authorities with varying types and amounts of taxes in their area. Because of this "location fixity" and full traceability, it is possible to determine which local government is the beneficiary of tax revenue.

Thirdly, even spatial distribution of the tax base. Pursuing the demand to control the territorial differentiation of tax financial efficiency for most taxes is impossible. For instance, revenue from turnover and income taxes, which are strictly linked to diverse levels of their assessment base, exhibit flexibility, adapting to the evolving trends in the economy. This shows that the rational selection of local taxes only partially mitigates significant disparities between impoverished and affluent municipalities. Hence, when creating the local tax system, it should be borne in mind (due to the social importance of local government tasks) that it is necessary to develop an appropriate compensatory mechanism at the national level.

The literature shows the characteristics of a desirable and optimal local tax system. B. Guziejewska claims that the effectiveness of such a system should be related to ensuring sufficient revenue to finance municipal tasks and enhancing local democracy, as well as in the context of fostering the identification of specific preferences of residents (2016). This approach thus integrates the correlation between the amount of local tax burdens and the level of municipal services while also accounting for residents' preferences within the constraints of public system resources.

Therefore, the local tax system should generate revenues that allow local government authorities to deliver public services at an adequate level. An efficient system should contribute to the improvement of the quality of life of residents and the promotion of sustainability in municipalities. It should be emphasised that in light of the fiscal principles of taxation (efficiency, flexibility, constancy), property taxes are regarded positively (Głuszak and Marona 2015). Irrespective of the type of tax (area-based system, classic property tax, mixed property tax, land tax), it is an efficient source of revenue. The area-based system is flexible, as tax rates can be varied to adapt to evolving economic circumstances. Revenues from the area-based system are also stable and predictable, as confirmed by the data for Polish local units. Value-based property tax meets the criteria of efficiency and flexibility. However, there is a tremendous potential for variability compared to the area-based tax, as property value inherently fluctuates more than its size. Due to its narrower (confined to land) tax base, the land tax performs less effectively in this assessment.

In addition to their fiscal function, local taxes also serve non-fiscal roles related to democratising social life and civic participation (Guziejewska 2016). The non-fiscal roles of local taxes can be contrasted with the purpose of local governments. Consequently, local government authorities can use property taxes to achieve various objectives, including efficient property utilisation, shaping a rational spatial structure of urban and rural areas, encouraging environmentally friendly behaviours and more efficient use of environmental resources (supporting environmental protection). Local government units, as entities of fiscal policy, affect socio-economic phenomena. The tasks conducted through local fiscal policy mean, therefore:

- satisfaction with the local government's demand for financial resources, accounting for the financial efficiency of local taxes;
- pursuit of statutory tasks of the local government bodies when using the collected revenues;
- meeting non-fiscal objectives of local governments through tax policy tools.

Property tax is seen as a favourable solution for local governments, with attention drawn, for example, to its fairness (the relation to the local services received), the difficulty of avoiding it, and the support of local autonomy and financial responsibility. What is crucial for residents is the connection between locally funded services (from property taxes), such as good schools, access to roads, pavements and other infrastructure, and their beneficial impact on property values (Fischel 2001). On the other hand, the fact that it is essentially impossible to evade such taxes is advantageous for the local government. After all, the location of a property cannot be changed in response to taxation; it cannot be hidden. The immovability of property is precisely the feature that makes property a desirable tax base in the local tax system. Property taxation can be seen as an essential instrument of local autonomy, but only when not used by other levels of government and if tax rates are set only at the local level (Slack 2011).

2.2 The idea and systematics of property taxes

Property tax is a permanent element within a modern local government revenue system. However, its fiscal significance varies in different countries due to several factors (Felis 2014).

Firstly, as discussed in the preceding subchapter, due to different perceptions of the scope of local government responsibilities. The primary duty of local governments is to ensure the uninterrupted provision of public goods and services. Their activities, however, should not be limited to public utilities but also affect the environment and supporting its socio-economic development.

Secondly, as already mentioned, individual countries have various categories of local taxes. For instance, property taxes predominate in Australia, Canada, Mexico, and the United States within the revenue structure of local governments in federal states. In contrast, property taxes carry the most significant weight in the local government revenue structure in unitary states such as the United Kingdom, New Zealand, the Netherlands, and France.

Thirdly, modern property taxation systems are diverse and include those based on property value as determined in property cadastres and those whose tax base is the property area. Moreover, practical challenges associated with property tax cannot be ignored, including tax base erosion and improper management. The erosion of the tax base, stemming from various tax preferences, requires increasing tax rates to maintain the proper revenue level. However, higher tax rates typically result in increased fiscal costs, including costs borne by taxpayers (so-called adaptation costs), and reduce the overall efficiency of the tax system. Management and administration represent vital elements concerning the tax revenue amount and the tax system's fairness and efficiency. For instance, fair and efficient value-based property taxes necessitate credible initial property valuations and periodic updates to reflect changes in property values.

Property taxation includes several types of levies. First of all, fixed property taxes and transactional property taxes should be distinguished. Fixed property taxes typically entail annual payments by property owners or users and are calculated based on the adopted measure of the property's value, which is periodically updated. At the same time, transaction taxes are levied on property sales or other transfers. Despite some standard features, applying fixed and transaction property taxes leads to different economic and social consequences. Given the subject of this monograph, it is limited to presenting the economic and social consequences of applying fixed property taxes (Felis 2013).

Fixed property taxes cause distortions of the market mechanism in the field of decisions concerning the choice between current and future consumption, as well as decisions concerning the structure of production and the structure of the factors used. However, assessing their impact on economic choices is difficult, as it depends on the structure of real property assets (land, buildings). It is worth paying particular attention to the mobility of production factors and the elasticity of demand and supply of the taxed factor. This applies, for example, to land whose resources are limited, which results in the creation of planning rents. As a result, taxation of the land, in part attributable to its value, burdens the rent.

Fixed property taxes are highly predictable, which is vital for the sustainability of public finances. These taxes can be attributed to a particular immanent feature – the rigid nature of the reaction of influences to changes in the market situation. The value of the property, valued and entered in the cadastral register, shows natural resistance to flexible, automatic adaptation to changes in the market situation. A high degree of stability of budget revenues facilitates budget planning. This is also important for investment activity and rationalisation of the financial management of the local government sector. However, one cannot overlook the specific cyclical nature of this type of levies (e.g. the tendency to increase the tax burden in the phase of falling prices) caused by the lack of immediate and complete updating of the property valuation.

With fixed property taxes, tax justice is implemented more favourably for taxpayers. However, the condition for meeting the standards of justice in real property taxation is the adoption of a valuable tax assessment base, thanks to which it will be possible to coincide between the amount of the tax burden and the degree of actual ability to bear the tax. It is also essential to introduce a complete and consistent cadastral system, honest estimation of the value of real property, and proper management and administration of the cadastral system. It should be expected that negligence in this area, for example, the lack of or occasional updates of the valuation of real property and infrequent and ineffective inspections of the condition of real property, will adversely affect the efficiency and fairness of the *ad valorem tax*.

Among the countries in which fixed property taxes are in force, significant differences in their structure are observed, concerning, for example, the choice of the tax base (valuation based on market value, land value, and rental value and based on unit value, i.e. the unit area of real property) as well as the determination of tax rates (uniform or variable tax rates; the entity responsible for determining the tax rates – at the level of central or local level).

Moreover, divisions should also be remembered according to the taxpayer category, i.e. the division into households (using residential real property) and enterprises (using business real property). Hence, when writing about a fixed property tax, one should bear in mind two different taxes: residential real property and non-residential (commercial) real property.

The need to examine the taxation of business real property (commercial and industrial) and residential real property is justified in the context of the planes of distortion of the market mechanism by distorting taxes and the role of the tax at the local level. Real property owned by entrepreneurs is used as a production factor in the production process; hence, their taxation leads to a distortion of the structure of production factors. Such consequences will not occur if residential real property is burdened.

Property tax – as mentioned in the previous subchapter – can be assigned certain features considered desirable for local taxes, which is why it is treated in most European countries as the most common local tax. Among the features that should be met by taxes constituting the essential revenue capacity of local governments, the following should be indicated: even distribution of the tax base, territorial unambiguity, permanent spatial relationship of the tax base, and tax visibility (which ensures public responsibility and transparency). What is important here is the specificity of real property as a category of sources of own revenue at the local level, i.e. its diversity, strong connection with a specific place (immobility), and durability over time (longevity). Due to these arguments, as well as the relationship between the types of services financed at the local level and the resulting benefit for the value of real property, property tax is a suitable solution for the financial management of local governments. However, there are severe doubts as to whether the role of taxes on residential and non-residential real property can be assessed in the same way because each tax imposed on production factors corrects the market decision of the producer, adjusting the volume and structure of production to tax rationality (Grądalski 2006). Hence, the literature emphasises that although many economic arguments for the residential property tax can be cited, the same cannot be said about the commercial real property tax (Slack 2011). The imposition of high property taxes on entrepreneurs may give rise to the inhibition of investment and modernisation processes. They pose a potential risk of triggering a tendency to an unjustified process of liquidation of a part of fixed assets, which periodically – for several reasons – cannot be productively engaged. And this means severe market distortions of entrepreneurs' decisions, who often undertake irrational and costly adjustment reactions. However, it turns out that despite such an assessment, in most countries where property taxes are collected, real property related to business activity is charged higher rates than others.[1] Consequently, this implies some doubts about economic efficiency and fairness.

2.3 Theoretical concepts of real property tax

The place of property taxes in the local tax system is still the subject of economic considerations and debates. However, their assessment is not unambiguous – two different theoretical concepts have been formed: the theory of benefits[2] and the theory of capital.[3] According to the benefit theory, local property tax is a tax paid in exchange for providing local public services. On the other hand, in the second – the capital concept, it is a distorting tax, most often leading to ineffective allocation of capital in local jurisdictions.

In the perspective of benefits developed by B.W. Hamilton, the property tax plays the role of the poll tax, provided for in the model of the efficiency of local public services provided by Tiebout (1956). In his model, Hamilton made specific assumptions, such as combining units into local jurisdictions according to the demand for public services, a certain number of districts within a larger agglomeration providing various public services, excellent consumer mobility to use public services, and the use of mandatory spatial planning restrictions by communities. According to B.W. Hamilton, these assumptions are sufficient to create a balance in which all communities are homogeneous (both in terms of public services and types of residential properties). As we know, the total homogeneity of property values within all communities is unrealistic, which is why, in subsequent studies, Hamilton expands the logic of the perspective of benefits, allowing communities that are heterogeneous in terms of property value (although remaining homogeneous in terms of demand for public services). A broader scope of the study showed that in a non-homogeneous community, the differences between public service benefits and tax burdens are capitalised in the price of real property. According to Hamilton, achieving adequate public services will be possible if local governments can issue spatial planning regulations.[4] The spatial planning tools used to implement fiscal policy, therefore, reduce to a certain minimum level the value of residential buildings that can be erected in the region. With such a minimum value, the revenues from real property taxation will exactly balance the value of the public services obtained. Similar conclusions can be found in the works of W.A. Fischel (1975) and M.J. White (1975), in which the authors focused on the issues of taxation of commercial and industrial real property, thus expanding the scope of the perspective of benefits.

A review of the results of the theoretical considerations conducted by B.W. Hamilton (1975) enables the formulation of the following conclusions regarding the role of the property tax from the perspective of benefits:

- property tax as an effective fee for the use of local public services does not lead to distortions of the consumption of residential real property and the level of public services provided,
- replacement of local property taxes with other, typical taxes at the national level will reduce the efficiency.

P. Mieszkowski and G.R. Zodrow (1986), representatives of the second trend (new, capital perspective), criticise the consideration of the local property tax from the perspective of benefits, claiming that unrealistic assumptions regarding spatial planning (its extensiveness and obligation) have been adopted. The capital perspective is inscribed in the general equilibrium model with fixed national capital resources and two types of local jurisdictions, characterised by relatively high and low tax rates. P. Mieszkowski proved that the effect of property tax rates above the average level in the country would be the outflow of capital from jurisdictions with high taxes to jurisdictions with relatively low taxes. Thus, the differentiation of property tax leads to inefficient capital allocation in different jurisdictions. It should also be noted that the average burden of all property taxes imposed in the country is borne by the owners of capital (the so-called profit effect) and that local differences in profit compared to the national average burden consumers or suppliers of residential buildings. According to this perspective, introducing real property taxation should be progressive. According to P. Mieszkowski, the differentiation of the property tax also determines the so-called excise tax effect, which means that in jurisdictions with a higher tax, the prices of residential real property will be higher, and remuneration and land prices will be lower than in jurisdictions with relatively low taxes. Assuming that these more or less symmetrical effects of excise duty tend to cancel each other, according to G.R. Zodrow (2007), the effect of tax profit is the main factor affecting the distribution of the tax burden in the capital perspective. According to the cited economist, if it is assumed that this perspective is correct, then replacing local property taxes with any typical tax instrument at the national level will have a variable impact on efficiency. It will depend on how the costs of efficiency, misallocation of capital, and insufficient provision of public services within real property tax relate to those under the selected tax instrument at a national level.

The following conclusions can be drawn from the discussed trend of research on real property tax:

- as a differentiated capital tax, it distorts the allocation of capital in local jurisdictions; in the case of residential real property, it distorts decisions on the consumption of residential real property;
- the use of property tax by local governments leads to reduced local public services, which prevents the outflow of mobile capital out of their jurisdiction (the problem of tax competition).

Summing up various implications of the presented theories of real property tax, it can be concluded that the economic effects of the capital perspective arise as a result of the tax-related reallocation of capital of residential real property. In contrast, from the perspective of benefits, such reallocations are prevented due to spatial planning restrictions or perfect capitalisation in the case of fully developed communities (Zodrow 2007).

The presented conclusions prompt us to ask about the possibility of reconciling two significantly different conceptual frameworks. One of the proposals is hybrid models attempting to combine the theory of the benefit perspective and the new perspective, creating a real chance of agreement in a long-term debate on which perspective better reflects the effects of the property tax. Hybrid models are classified into the following groups: hybrid models with non-mobile residents, hybrid models with perfectly mobile residents, and the inter-jurisdictional capitalisation model. G.R. Zodrow sees great value in these models – in his opinion, all hybrid perspectives. However, they are significantly closer to the capital perspective than the benefit perspective, coming from the perspective of benefits (2007). The economist points to two ways of future empirical research to determine the degree:

- to which actual land-use constraints are binding for marginal decisions on residential real property;
- in which relatively high property taxes reduce the practical consumption of residential real property or reduce the capital intensity of residential and non-residential production, in line with the capital perspective.

It is also worth mentioning another proposal, according to which the research trend should also focus on the strategic choice, which is tantamount to using models in which game theory would be used to map local government and other entities (Mandell 2001). It cannot be ruled out that new theoretical models will be constructed and more sophisticated empirical research will be conducted.

Summing up the output of leading real property tax researchers, it can be concluded that, despite the lack of consensus on many issues, both approaches (benefit-based and capital tax-based) are of great value. Therefore, it should be assumed that we are dealing with a tax that cannot be said to be a pure tax on benefits because by improving them, property owners will be burdened with a higher tax and thus discouraged from any investments. At the same time, the benefits of local socio-economic programmes are reflected in the value of local real property.

2.4 Property tax as a subject of economic reflection

Taxation is inevitable, as it provides funds to finance spending needs. However, taxation entails additional social costs and generally leads to distortions in the market system. Therefore, the tax system should be designed rationally. The key criterion for assessing the tax system is its effectiveness, largely a derivative of neutrality.

According to the theory of optimal taxation, the tax system should be as neutral as possible concerning the market mechanism (Grądalski 2006). This is one of the critical principles of rationalising the tax system, according to which tax solutions should be applied that distort the rules of the market mechanism as little as possible (distort the areas of microeconomic market choices that are important for achieving state policy objectives). Complete neutrality, i.e. identical tax treatment of similar activities, goods, incomes, and assets, is impossible. However, the tax system should be designed in such a way as to reduce the possibilities of arbitrage and limit the phenomenon of tax avoidance and evasion.

A neutral real property tax system is one in which taxation does not distort the functioning of the real property market. Of course, this is unrealistic because real property taxes affect the market and decisions made by investors, developers, and users.

As emphasised before, property taxes are not uniform. They are fixed property taxes and transaction taxes on real property. Although they have some standard features, they differ significantly regarding economic and social effects. Depending on their types, they lead to the formation of various distortions (Felis 2012).

Firstly, in decisions concerning the choice between current and future consumption. The property tax is an example of a burden on future consumption, which, depending on its amount, may discourage entrepreneurs from accumulating and developing. The impact on possible shifts of individual preferences in favour of current consumption also depends on the amount of its burden. At the same time, it should be remembered that in the case of residential real property, which does not have a substitute, the fixed tax is included in their maintenance costs. This means that the amount of the tax will not affect the purchase decision but may only affect the decision to choose a residential unit – its area, structure, and location (depending on the type of tax applied). The choice of renting instead of owning is only an indirect escape towards consumption, as it is customary for property owners to pass on at least part of the costs to the tenant (in the case of fixed property tax, this is not an explicit element of the rent). Ultimately, the amount of the tax also affects the market, as the developer decides on the structure of multi-apartment construction mainly based on demand.

Secondly, in the area of decisions concerning the choice of the structure of immovable property (land, buildings). The mobility of production factors and the elasticity of demand and supply of the taxed factor are essential here. The burden of wealth taxes may apply to immobile factors of production, e.g. land. Its resources are limited, which results in the creation of planning rents. As a result, land taxation, partly attributable to its value, burdens the rent. Due to the inelasticity of the land supply, the burden of the wealth tax will be borne by the landowners. The tax will then be fully reflected in the decrease in the value of the land (the so-called capitalisation of the tax on the property price). Other consequences occur for factors of production characterised by elastic supply. In the long run, the supply of buildings is flexible, so investors, when given a choice of where to invest, make decisions based on the rate of return on investment after tax, considering the wealth taxes imposed. Of course, withdrawing capital may be difficult or even impossible in some fixed assets. High taxation will, therefore, limit new investments.

Undoubtedly, the method of taxation of individual types of immovable property is also essential here. Any differentiation of tax rates (area-based tax, value-based tax, and non-taxation of certain types of immovable property) affects decisions regarding the use of individual factors of production. A different tax treatment of immovable assets causes distortions in the taxpayer's choice of asset type. One way to minimise the adverse tax effects may be arbitration between various kinds of immovable property, which are treated differently regarding taxes. Tax avoidance can consist of choosing an alternative form of tax on land: real property, agricultural, or forestry. As in Poland, preferential taxation of agricultural and forest land compared to other land may cause taxpayers to escape from paying property tax in favour of other, more advantageous levies. Let us also note that by choosing the structure of assets, which is concretised in the most favourable taxation for him, the entrepreneur creates the basis for creating criteria alien to the market mechanism. These criteria force taxpayers to reorient their activities from economically effective behaviours to behaviours aimed at reducing property taxes. Such actions lead to additional losses in prosperity on a macroeconomic scale. This problem is also raised at the level of real property valuation, where the market value should always result not so much from the actual use of the real property as from its most helpful function (*the principle of highest and best use*). When calculating the tax on the value of real property, which is estimated based on its actual function, there may be significant differences between the cadastral and market values. And this has further consequences related to financing (mortgage security) or sale.

On the other hand, transaction taxes imposed on real property, mainly when they constitute a significant part of sales costs, adversely affect the efficiency and size of the real property market. High transaction taxes may discourage transactions in the real property market. Consequently, this freezes investors' portfolios, thus discouraging active management of investment assets, contributing to market stagnation and limited exchanges. Moreover, additional barriers between the transaction participants cause real property market imbalances, which may spill over into other markets (e.g. hindering labour mobility).

Considering the possible reactions of taxpayers to the taxation of real property, it should be emphasised that fixed real property taxes are – if the real property register is prepared correctly – more difficult to circumvent than transaction taxes. In response to them, entities undertake specific tax evasion tactics, such as undercutting transaction prices. From the point of view of the market, it is a very harmful practice, also at the level of estimating the market value of real property in general. If determined using a comparative approach, this results from actual transaction prices. If underestimated, they present a distorted market picture, ultimately affecting other transactions. Taxes levied on real property turnover may also constitute a significant breach of the principle of fair distribution of the tax burden. It is challenging to justify economic punishment for the behaviour of entities active on the market.

When considering the problem of property tax neutrality in detail, it is necessary to consider the different systems of collecting real property tax. Using the following criteria: location, development intensity, and development time in specific real property taxation solutions, it can be assumed that (Głuszak and Marona 2015):

- classic property tax is not a neutral tax (all three criteria indicate this);
- mixed tax and area tax cause more disputes among researchers (some consider them neutral but under certain conditions);
- of all the solutions, the land tax is the closest to neutrality (this is indicated by two criteria: location and intensity of development).

The theory of taxation generally leads to the conclusion that the tax on land value is neutral. Above all, its neutrality concerning the economic use of land is emphasised. This was pointed out by D. Netzer, who stated that

> the planning rent on the location is a surplus, and its taxation will not limit the supply of the resources offered; taxation of land value will be completely neutral with regard to the decisions of landowners, since there is no possible response to taxation that could improve their situation, assuming that landowners used their resources to the maximum extent before the introduction of taxation.
>
> (1966)

According to some theorists, B.L. Bentick (1979) and D.E. Mills (1981), the taxation of land value will not necessarily be neutral about the moment of implementation and the nature of the investment. Their models showed that land value taxation could influence the choice between earlier and later investment in unused land in favour of projects that generate earlier net income streams. A shift towards land taxation may, therefore, accelerate investment, even to an excessive extent, from the point of view of economic efficiency. This effect, called the time effect, depends on the fulfilment of essential but controversial assumptions underlying the determination of the value of land for tax purposes.

When it comes to the classic property tax, there is no doubt – it is not a neutral tax. According to D.E. Mills, quoted above, the classic property value tax is not neutral because:

1 tax reduces the propensity to invest (the higher the value of building improvements, the higher the tax);

2 it encourages high-income construction investments in the initial period of operation and discourages long-term, profitable investments in the future.

To recap the considerations concerning the economic effects of real property tax burdens, it should be emphasised that the real property taxation system should include solutions that ensure efficient sources of financing of local public needs and those that do not interfere with the development of the real sphere. Exceeding a specific limit by the legislator may, in some situations, even contribute to the disposal of immovable property and thus to its decapitalisation.

Notes

1 An example to quote is the research of R.M. Bird and E. Slack, who analysed local and wealth tax systems in 25 countries. It turned out that in the vast majority of cases the tax rate on non-residential properties was higher than the tax rate on residential property (2004).
2 The theory of considering the local property tax as a tax on benefits was developed by B.W. Hamilton (1975).
3 This concept was created by P. Mieszkowski and H.J. Aaron, among others, and was later developed by G. R. Zodrow and P. Mieszkowski (Aaron 1975; Mieszkowski 1972; Zodrow and Mieszkowski 1986).
4 Thanks to spatial planning restrictions, it will be impossible to have "free rides" at the expense of neighbours, such as building a small, inexpensive house in a prestigious part of the city with large, expensive houses, and thus using public goods that have been paid for to a large extent by others.

Bibliography

Aaron, Henry J. 1975. *Who Pays the Property Tax? A New View. Studies of Government Finance Second Series*. Washington, DC: The Brookings Institution.

Bahl, Roy W., and Richard M. Bird. 2008. "Subnational Taxes in Developing Countries: The Way Forward." *Institute for International Business Working Paper*, no. 16. doi:10.2139/ssrn.1273753.

Bentick, Brian L. 1979. "The Impact of Taxation and Valuation Practices on the Timing and Efficiency of Land Use." *Journal of Political Economy* 87 (4): 859–868.

Bird, Richard, and Enid Slack. 2004. *International Handbook of Land and Property Taxation*. Cheltenham: Edward Elgar Publishing.

Felis, Paweł. 2012. *Elementy teorii i praktyki podatków majątkowych: poszukiwanie ładu w opodatkowaniu nieruchomości w Polsce z perspektywy przedsiębiorców oraz jednostek samorządu terytorialnego*. Monografie i Opracowania/Szkoła Główna Handlowa 588. Warszawa: Oficyna Wydawnicza SGH – Szkoła Główna Handlowa.

Felis, Paweł. 2013. "Opodatkowanie majątku w Europie - współczesne trendy i wyzwania." In *Wiedza i bogactwo narodów. Kapitał ludzki, globalizacja i regulacja w skali światowej. Ekonomia i finanse*, edited by Ryszard Bartkowiak and Piotr Wachowiak, 87–97. Warszawa: Oficyna Wydawnicza SGH.

Felis, Paweł. 2014. "Główne koncepcje podatku od nieruchomości." In *Finanse w polityce makroekonomicznej państwa*, edited by Stanisław Owsiak, 246–256. Kraków: Wydawnictwo Uniwersytetu Ekonomicznego w Krakowie.

Fischel, William A. 1975. "Fiscal and Environmental Considerations in the Location of Firms in Suburban Communities." In *Fiscal Zoning and Land Use Controls*, edited by Edwin S. Mills and Wallace E. Oates, 119–173. Lexington, MA: Lexington Books.

Fischel, William A. 2001. "Homevoters, Municipal Corporate Governance, and the Benefit View of the Property Tax." *National Tax Journal* 54 (1): 157–174.

Głuszak, Michał, and Bartlomiej Marona. 2015. *Podatek Katastralny. Ekonomiczne Uwarunkowania Reformy Opodatkowania Nieruchomości*. Warszawa: Wydawnictwo Poltext.

Grądalski, Feliks. 2006. *System Podatkowy w Świetle Teorii Optymalnego Opodatkowania*. Warszawa: Oficyna Wydawnicza SGH.

Guziejewska, Beata. 2016. "W Poszukiwaniu Efektywnego Sytemu Podatków Samorządowych." *Annales Universitatis Mariae Curie-Skłodowska, Sectio H, Oeconomia* 50 (1): 275. doi:10.17951/h.2016.50.1.275.

Hamilton, Bruce W. 1975. "Zoning and Property Taxation in a System of Local Governments." *Urban Studies* 12 (2): 205–211.

Karpus, Karolina. 2002. *Systemy podatków lokalnych w wybranych państwach europejskich*. Toruń: Adam Marszałek.

Kornberger-Sokołowska, Elżbieta. 2001. *Decentralizacja finansów publicznych a samodzielność finansowa jednostek samorządu terytorialnego*. Warszawa: Liber.

Korolewska, Monika. 2021. "Samorządowe Dochody Podatkowe w Wybranych Państwach Unii Europejskiej." *Studia BAS* 1 (65): 251–282. doi:10.31268/StudiaBAS.2021.13.

Mandell, Svante. 2001. *Ground Leases & Local Property Taxes*. Stockholm: Department of Real Estate and Construction Management, Royal Institute of Technology.

Mieszkowski, Peter. 1972. "The Property Tax: An Excise Tax or a Profits Tax?" *Journal of Public Economics* 1 (1): 73–96. doi:10.1016/0047-2727(72)90020-5.

Mills, David E. 1981. "The Non-Neutrality of Land Value Taxation." *National Tax Journal* 34 (1): 125–129. doi:10.1086/NTJ41862356.

Netzer, Dick. 1966. *Economics of the Property Tax*. Washington, DC: The Brookings Institution.

Slack, Enid. 2011. *The Property Tax - In Theory and Practice*. IMFG Papers on Municipal Finance and Governance, Toronto.

Swianiewicz, Paweł. 2004. *Finanse Lokalne. Teoria i Praktyka*. Warszawa: Municipium.

Tiebout, Charles M. 1956. "A Pure Theory of Local Expenditures." *Journal of Political Economy* 64 (5): 416–424.

White, Michelle J. 1975. "Firm Location in a Zoned Metropolitan Area." In *Fiscal Zoning and Land Use Controls*, edited by Edwin S. Mills and Wallace E. Oates, 31–101. Lexington, MA: Lexington Books.

Wyszkowska, Dorota. 2017. "Samodzielność Dochodowa Jednostek Samorządu Terytorialnego - Polska Na Tle Wybranych Krajów Unii Europejskiej." *Annales Universitatis Mariae Curie-Skłodowska, Sectio H, Oeconomia* 51 (5): 371. doi:10.17951/h.2017.51.5.371.

Zodrow, George R. 2007. "The Property Tax Incidence Debate and the Mix of State and Local Finance of Local Public Expenditures." *CESifo Economic Studies* 53 (4): 495–521.

Zodrow, George R., and Peter M. Mieszkowski. 1986. "The New View of the Property Tax A Reformulation." *Regional Science and Urban Economics* 16 (3): 309–327. doi:10.1016/0166-0462(86)90028-1.

3 Fiscal capacity of area-based real estate taxes in selected countries of Central and Eastern Europe

3.1 Real estate tax in local budgets' structure

By ensuring fiscal autonomy on levels below the central one, fiscal decentralisation is seen as an instrument to improve the efficiency of public services provision. It also empowers local governments to undertake activities supporting local economic development. It is believed that fiscal decentralisation indirectly influences the pace of economic growth, although empirical evidence concerning this influence is not entirely clear, both about its direction and its power (Baskaran and Feld 2013; Thornton 2007; Mauro, Pigliaru, and Carmeci 2018). As stated by Bahl (1999), fiscal decentralisation requires significant local government taxing powers, and according to Shah (1994), assigning tax sources to various government levels should be based on effective administration and fiscal needs criteria. Shah (1994) states that taxes related to mobile factors (PIT, CIT, and others) should contribute to the central budget, while taxes related to immobile factors (such as real estate tax) should be the source of local government revenue.

Taxes that generate local budget revenue include local taxes – in the case of which local authorities have certain (varied) degrees of taxing power – and so-called shared taxes that are imposed and collected by higher tier authorities, although partially transferred to local government units (LGUs) budgets. Such shared taxes may be allocated between LGUs according to their share in generating revenue (individual proportionality) (Blöchliger and Petzold 2009, 4). Still, they may also form a part of equalising mechanisms – the lower the unit's resources, the larger the transfers of funds from shared taxes (Dougherty, Harding, and Reschovsky 2019, 7). How these shares are determined (OECD 2021, 83) will also impact the tax autonomy of LGUs. Nevertheless, LGU revenue from shared taxes does not depend solely on how their shares are decided since the main elements of these taxes (Pest 2014) and the macroeconomic circumstances also contribute significantly.

Pursuant to the European Charter of Local Self-Government (1985), at least part of the financial resources of local authorities shall derive from local taxes and charges of which, within the statutory limits, they have the power

DOI: 10.4324/9781003530503-4

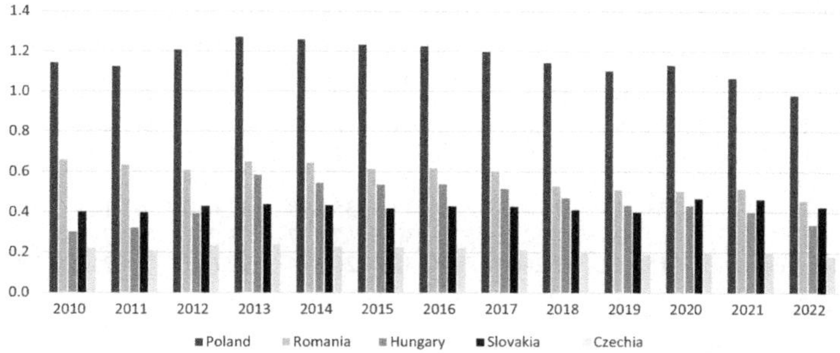

Figure 3.1 Real estate tax revenue as % of GDP in selected CEE countries.

Source: European Commission, DG Taxation and Customs Union, based on Eurostat data (European Commission 2023).

to determine the rate. One of the essential sources of revenue is the real estate tax, which is deemed stable and predictable – real estate ownership is usually easy to determine, and its fixed geographical location makes tax evasion difficult (Leodolter, Princen, and Rutkowski 2022).

While many European Union countries employ an ad valorem tax base, the methods for determining this value vary considerably across nations. The variance extends to valuation procedures and, for instance, entities in charge of conducting valuations and the frequency of property revaluations. In turn, several Central and Eastern European (CEE) countries rely on alternative approaches. In countries such as Poland, Romania, Hungary, Slovakia, and Czechia, as analysed below, real estate taxation primarily revolves around an area-based system, albeit with occasional incorporation of property values.

In 2010–2022, revenue from real estate tax accounted, on average, for 3.1% of total taxation in the European Union. The highest ratios were noted in France, Greece, and Denmark, while in CEE countries with area-based systems – in Poland. Among the countries that use area-based real estate taxation, Poland stands out also in terms of the ratio of this tax revenue to GDP, which is, on average, 1.2%. The second largest ratio (in Romania) is half as much. The lowest ratio was observed in Czechia, where real estate tax revenue accounts for only 0.2% of GDP (Figure 3.1).

In Poland, the real estate tax is the most essential local tax. Revenue from this tax in 2010 amounted to PLN 15.1 billion, rising to PLN 28.1 billion in 2022. The average growth pace of real estate tax revenue was 5.1%, although, since 2014, it has been growing slower than its revenue. In Poland, own revenue comes mainly from sources which do not depend on local authorities, such as shares in tax revenue (PIT and CIT) (Table 3.1).

The considerable fiscal importance of real estate tax is evidenced by its average share in Polish municipal own revenue, which was 22.0% (37.4%

Table 3.1 Revenue of Polish municipalities in the years 2010–2022 (in million PLN)

	2010	*2012*	*2014*	*2016*	*2018*	*2020*	*2022*
Total revenue	126,196	139,654	152,809	176,215	206,933	249,405	282,010
Own revenue	66,548	73,931	84,605	91,004	104,942	121,693	145,799
Of which:							
- PIT	23,215	26,486	30,148	35,275	43,640	47,143	57,292
- CIT	2,025	2,252	2,130	2,477	3,241	3,792	5,052
- Real estate tax	15,122	17,603	19,532	20,774	22,617	24,216	28,058
- Civil law transactions tax	1,893	1,492	1,798	2,172	2,748	3,005	4,154
Grants	25,168	27,794	30,054	44,369	58,249	77,309	80,117
General subvention	34,480	37,930	38,150	40,842	43,743	50,403	56,094

Source: own study based on Ministry of Finance Republic of Poland data (Ministerstwo Finansów 2023).

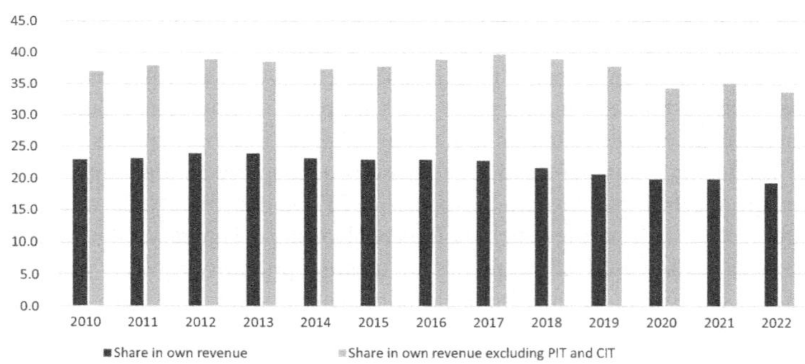

Figure 3.2 Share of the real estate tax in own revenue of municipalities and own revenue excluding the shared taxes in Poland in the years 2010–2022 (in %).

Source: own study based on Ministry of Finance Republic of Poland data (Ministerstwo Finansów 2023).

when excluding the shared taxes from own revenue). The highest value of the measure was noted in 2013 and 2014 (both 23.8%) and the lowest in 2022 (19.2%). If we consider own revenue without shares in PIT and CIT, the highest ratio was 39.6% (2017), and the lowest was 33.6% (2022) (see Figure 3.2).

The importance of the real estate tax varies depending on the kind of municipality. As of 2024, there are 2,477 municipalities in Poland. This figure includes urban municipalities (some of which belong to the additional category of cities with county rights), urban-rural municipalities and rural municipalities, the latter of which are the most numerous (1,464 units). The highest

Table 3.2 Real estate tax revenue and its share in own revenue and total revenue in the years 2010–2022 in Poland, by type of municipality

	2010	*2012*	*2014*	*2016*	*2018*	*2020*	*2022*
Real estate tax (in million PLN)							
Cities with county rights	6,062	6,995	7,701	8,148	8,817	9,227	10,610
Urban municipalities	2,616	3,039	3,233	3,391	3,611	3,855	4,410
Urban-rural municipalities	3,285	3,868	4,315	4,643	5,151	5,637	6,636
Rural municipalities	3,160	3,701	4,284	4,592	5,039	5,498	6,402
Share of real estate tax in own revenue (in %)							
Cities with county rights	17.7	18.7	18.0	17.8	16.8	16.5	16.0
Urban municipalities	27.1	28.8	27.8	27.1	25.0	23.2	22.8
Urban-rural municipalities	29.8	30.4	29.7	29.3	27.8	24.5	23.8
Cities with county rights	17.7	18.7	18.0	17.8	16.8	16.5	16.0
Share of real estate tax in total revenue (in %)							
Cities with county rights	11.2	11.4	11.3	10.9	10.3	9.2	9.6
Urban municipalities	15.8	17.2	17.0	15.0	13.4	11.9	12.6
Urban-rural municipalities	13.7	14.7	15.2	13.4	12.4	11.0	11.1
Rural municipalities	9.9	10.7	11.6	10.3	9.5	8.4	8.3

Source: Own study based on Ministry of Finance Republic of Poland data (Ministerstwo Finansów 2023).

share of real estate tax revenue in own revenue was recorded in urban-rural municipalities, with 28.1% on average in 2010–2022, while the lowest share was observed in cities with county rights (17.3%). Analysing the structure of total municipality revenue, one can notice that real estate tax is most important for urban municipalities (14.8% of revenue on average) and least important for rural municipalities (9.9%) (Table 3.2).

Romanian local governments have minimal revenue sources, with more than 80% of their total revenue deriving from transfers in the form of grants and subsidies (European Commission 2022, 13). Substantial local taxes include property taxes levied on immobile structures (buildings, land) and mobile objects (vehicles).

Revenue from immovable property tax grew considerably from RON 1,479 million to RON 6,133 million between 2005 and 2021. This revenue is dominated by the tax on buildings, which accounts for almost three-fourths of the total, with the tax on buildings held by legal persons playing a decisively important role (Figure 3.3).

The share of tax on buildings in the local budgets varies widely. In the case of tax paid by natural persons, the ratios are generally lower (1%–6%), and the spread between individual municipalities is also smaller. Much larger spreads, up to a dozen and more percentage points, can be observed in the case of tax paid by legal persons, especially when small and large municipalities are compared (Spatari 2020).

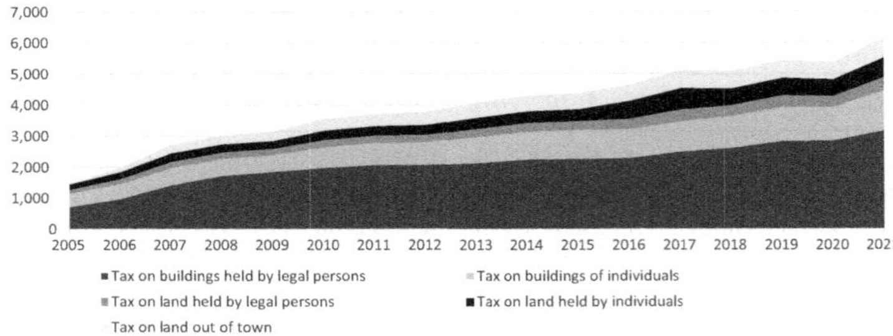

Figure 3.3 Recurrent taxes on immovable property in Romania in 2005–2021 (in million RON).

Source: European Commission, DG Taxation and Customs Union, based on Eurostat data (European Commission 2023).

In Hungary, the local revenue structure strictly depends on organisational and financial changes introduced in the local government system. Real estate taxes (on land and buildings) are introduced only in a small part of municipalities. Nevertheless, in 2010–2022, revenue from that source was, on average, equal to 16.3% of local tax revenue and 4.5% of total local revenue. In nominal terms, real estate tax receipts increased significantly. At the start of the analysed period, they were equal to HUF 82 billion, 2.6% of total local revenue. Since 2019, their amounts have exceeded HUF 150 billion, accounting for about 5% of total revenue (Table 3.3).

In Slovakia, real estate tax is the most essential local tax. Municipalities also impose other taxes, including dog tax, accommodation tax, tax on vending machines, nuclear facility tax, and a tax on the entry and stay of motor vehicles in historical parts of towns.

From 2012 to 2022, the real estate tax revenue of Slovak municipalities grew by one-half, from EUR 304 million to EUR 457 million (Table 3.4). The pace of growth of this revenue was usually slower than the growth of total municipal tax revenue; however, in 2020, when total tax revenue increased by merely 1.8%, real estate tax revenue noted a surge of more than 17%. Nonetheless, a noticeable decrease in the fiscal importance of real estate tax can be observed. While at the beginning of the analysed period, receipts from this source accounted for 18.2% of tax revenue and 8.2% of total municipal revenue, in 2022, the percentages were, respectively, 14.2% and 6.7%. The real estate tax consists of the land tax, tax on buildings, and apartments tax. The tax on buildings is the most significant, generating about 70% of all real estate tax revenue, with the apartment tax being the least important and accounting for 6%–8% of revenue in recent years.

Czechia has the lowest fiscal importance of real estate tax, amounting to less than CZK 5 billion in 2007 and remaining at a similar level in the next year. In 2009, a change occurred, with real estate tax receipts growing by

Table 3.3 Revenue of the local government sector in Hungary (in million HUF)

	2010	*2012*	*2014*	*2016*	*2018*	*2020*	*2022*
Total revenue	3,169,694	2,801,638	2,996,126	2,261,752	2,819,125	3,155,114	3,741,588
Of which:							
Taxes and net social contribution	654,169	689,714	698,131	805,446	923,664	906,076	1,092,423
- Local business tax	443,093	471,031	523,125	608,982	711,276	729,000	890,118
- Real estate taxes	82,401	113,871	123,158	139,641	149,442	156,697	168,499
- Other taxes	128,675	104,812	51,848	56,823	62,946	20,379	33,806

Source: Own study based on data from the Hungarian Central Statistical Office (2024a, 2024b).

Table 3.4 Revenue of Slovak municipalities in 2012–2022 (in million EUR)

	2012	*2014*	*2016*	*2018*	*2020*	*2022*
Total revenue	3,698	4,029	4,389	5,251	5,992	6,828
Of which						
Current revenue	2,880	3,288	3,747	4,237	4,881	5,493
Tax revenue	1,674	1,798	2,192	2,567	2,842	3,217
Of which: real estate tax	304	320	336	355	428	457
Non-tax revenue	347	542	511	523	448	572
Transfers	859	948	1,044	1,147	1,591	1,704

Source: Own study based on Ministry of Finance data in the Slovak Republic (2024).

Table 3.5 Revenue of Czech municipalities in 2010–2022 (in million CZK)

	2010	*2012*	*2014*	*2016*	*2018*	*2020*	*2022*
Total revenue	283,620	241,071	272,912	278,951	330,861	368,980	437,484
Tax revenue	142,886	145,535	170,087	190,751	226,220	230,852	295,638
Of which:							
- PIT	32,671	32,915	37,225	44,780	54,193	57,761	52,934
- CIT	32,262	33,179	39,289	45,762	46,638	43,572	68,815
- VAT	57,551	55,744	67,631	72,523	97,661	101,662	138,812
- Real estate tax	8,664	9,602	9,973	10,586	10,856	11,563	12,354
Non-tax revenue	27,182	28,790	32,288	30,337	32,179	36,056	47,640
Property revenue	12,769	8,743	6,110	7,801	7,426	6,986	9,722
Transfers	100,784	58,004	64,427	50,063	65,035	95,086	84,483

Source: Own study based on Czech Statistical Office data (2023).

almost 25% and nearly 40% in 2010 to reach CZK 8.7 billion. Since then, revenue growth has been relatively stable, although usually lower than the growth of total local tax revenue (Table 3.5).

In 2007–2022, the share of real estate tax in Czech municipalities' tax revenue was 5.1% on average, and the share in total municipal revenue amounted to 3.2%. The shares were at their highest in 2012 and 2013, when they amounted to more than 6% and almost 4%, respectively. In subsequent years, the fiscal importance of real estate tax diminished, except in the year 2020, when an increase in this revenue source was observed.

3.2 What are the exogenic factors affecting real estate tax revenue?

Fiscal capacity, understood as the capability of raising revenue from taxes (Ricciuti, Savoia, and Sen 2019), is dependent on multiple factors, some of which are within the competence of local authorities, while others are not. In the case of the real estate tax, local authorities usually have no control over introducing a tax and determining its main elements, although exceptions do occur (Hungary). Generally, lower tax revenue is generated in countries in which area-based systems are used. Suppose the tax base relies on surface area. In that case, the effects of inflation are not automatically taken into account, making it necessary to introduce an indexation mechanism, most frequently in the structure of tax rates. However, this solution does not always produce the expected results and is noticeable for taxpayers who perceive it as an increased tax burden. In the case of municipalities, the area-based system of real estate taxation means that the tax base is rigid and hampers revenue growth from this source. At the same time, it provides a loose (or no) connection to taxpayers' ability to pay. The area-based system disregards factors that could affect the tax base, reflecting the real estate's location, market conditions, and quality. This does not mean, however, that tax burdens do not vary depending on the type, location, and use of real estate, as the legislator may adjust the individual surface area of real estate or apply a complicated system of quota tax rates. The rate amounts can be determined by the type of the object of taxation (improved or unimproved land) and its purpose (for commercial use or not). However, imposing taxes on immovable property used for business activities can have a choking effect on fostering entrepreneurship and harm the national economy (Felis 2015a).

The basic principles and structural features of real estate taxation significantly vary among European countries, stemming from distinct economic, demographic, and political conditions. Historical and organisational factors also play a crucial role. These encompass the historically determined patterns of property ownership, long-standing tax solutions, and the effectiveness of property registration systems. When considering legal determinants that affect real estate tax revenue, the key point lies in the permissible scope of taxpayer burden (including its differentiation) and the degree of local government taxing power.

3.2.1 Main characteristic features of real estate taxation in analysed countries

This chapter explores the legislative solutions adopted in countries where real estate taxation primarily relies on an area-based system, albeit with some incorporation of the value approach. The analysis was presented alphabetically in the Visegrad countries (Czechia, Hungary, Poland, and Slovakia) and Romania.

In Czechia, real estate tax comprises two components: (1) land tax and (2) tax on buildings and units. The primary legal act governing real estate taxation is the 1992 Real Estate Tax Act (Česká Národní Rada 1992). This Act underwent significant amendments in 2024 as part of a comprehensive tax reform package. Generally, real estate taxes are paid by the property owners; however, in specific instances, lessees or users of the land, as well as tenants of buildings or premises, are responsible for payment.

Land tax pertains to land registered in the real property cadastre, and it primarily relies on the land's area, although its value may also be considered in some instances. The tax for agricultural land is calculated as the multiple of its area (measured in square metres) and the average land price determined by the Minister of Agriculture through a decree issued under the Real Estate Tax Act. For forestry land, the tax base is either the land price set by relevant price regulations or the actual land area. For other types of land, the tax base is the area in square metres. For tax purposes, the tax rate varies based on the land type classification. For building plots, the predetermined rate of CZK 3.5 per m^2 is further multiplied by a coefficient, primarily determined by the population of the municipality where the land is situated. The coefficient may undergo additional adjustments, either reductions or increases, at the discretion of municipalities.

Czech tax on buildings and units applies to completed or occupied real estate, including residential buildings, recreational structures, garages, and buildings or units for business purposes. The tax base is the built-up area in square metres, while for units, it is the adjusted area of the units. This adjusted area is calculated by multiplying the area in square metres by 1.22 or 1.20, depending on whether the units are situated within a residential building and include a share of the land. The basic tax rates for buildings may be adjusted upwards for structures with additional above-ground storeys. Typically, these rates span from CZK 3.5 to CZK 18 per m^2. However, the rates might be subject to further increases in specific cases. For properties like residential buildings, determining the tax liability entails employing coefficients similar to those applied to building plots. These coefficients vary depending on factors such as the number of inhabitants and may be adjusted by local authorities. Specific properties may be subject to higher tax rates, with increases possibly introduced independently of municipal decisions.

In Czechia, municipalities have the authority to establish a local coefficient, which multiplies the taxpayer's liability for both the land tax and the tax on buildings and units. As of 2024, this coefficient may range from 0.5 to 5 and apply to properties across the entire municipality or properties within a specific municipality area. However, the coefficient does not affect land categorised as selected agricultural land, permanent grassland, or unusable land. In the case of these lands, a local coefficient ranging between 0.5 and 1.5 is applied, with only one factor permissible for each land group. In 2024, an inflation coefficient was introduced to automatically index the tax liability in subsequent years (Stibůrková, Havel, and Malá 2023).

Czech legislation includes numerous exemptions and exclusions from real estate tax (land tax and tax on buildings and units), often contingent upon the property not being used for business activities. Some exemptions are also subject to time limitations. According to Radvan (2019), exemptions and exclusions are currently excessive, and abandoning or narrowing them down would be advisable.

The real estate tax in Hungary, regulated by the Local Taxes Act of 1990 (Országgyűlés 1990), formally consists of two components: a land tax and a building tax. While the law outlines the essential elements of these taxes, including their maximum rates, municipal authorities decide whether to introduce them. In 2019, approximately 16% of all municipalities adopted a land tax, with nearly a third implementing a building tax, primarily in larger municipalities (Hulkó and Pardavi 2022, 47).

Municipalities in Hungary serve as the local tax authorities responsible for property tax administration and also have the discretion to determine the tax base, which may be the area in square metres or the adjusted market value. Although the law establishes upper limits on tax rates, municipalities can increase area-based rates annually by the cumulative inflation rate.

The landowner pays Hungarian land tax; the taxable object is the land within the municipality's jurisdiction. The Local Taxes Act outlines various categories of land tax exemptions. The limits on the tax rate are set at HUF 200 per m^2 (adjusted for inflation to HUF 398 per m^2 in 2023) or 3% of the adjusted market value.

In Hungary, taxes on buildings apply to residential and non-residential buildings, encompassing all buildings and parts regardless of their function or use. The tax liability is imposed on the owner of the building (or part of the building). However, the taxable object may differ if the property is encumbered by a right to dispose of the property, such as a trustee's right or usufructuary's right, registered in the land register. Municipalities can select their tax base; however, it is essential to maintain a uniform tax base for both property taxes (Hulkó and Feher 2021, 156). The maximum tax rate on buildings is HUF 1,100 per m^2 (adjusted for inflation, HUF 2,191 per m^2 in 2023) or 3.6% of the adjusted market value.

According to Hungarian legislation, property used exclusively for health care by family doctors and buildings solely used for storing radioactive waste or burnt nuclear fuel, among others, are exempt from taxation. Tax exemptions also apply to the renovation of listed buildings. If such a building undergoes renovation, it (or premises within it) is exempt from tax for three consecutive tax years from the effective date of the building or renovation permit.

The structure of real estate tax in Poland was established in the early 1990s through the provisions of the Act on Local Taxes and Fees of 12 January 1991 (Sejm Rzeczpospolitej Polskiej 1991), although regulations about this levy date back to the 1950s. Poland's comprehensive property taxation system comprises real estate, agricultural, and forest taxes. Characteristics of these taxes are the primary focus on the taxable object, which is the possession of specific real estate types. The real estate tax encompasses the broadest and most complex scope of the subject matter, including land, buildings or their parts, and structures or their parts related to business activities.

The tax base is natural for land and buildings: the area for land and the usable area for buildings or their parts. However, calculating the usable area presents numerous challenges (e.g. Pahl 2009). The only aspect of real estate taxation based on the value formula is the taxation of structures. Nevertheless, this should not be interpreted as a standard real estate tax, where the property's value determines the tax amount. In Poland, the economic value of the assets, which reflects the price of the property obtainable on the market, is not considered. Instead, the depreciation method determines the revenue tax value (see Felis 2012).

In Poland, real estate tax rates can be fixed amount-based or percentage-based, depending on the nature of the tax base. Fixed amount-based rates are determined by the type of taxable objects (land, buildings) and their intended use (non-business, business, or preferred business activities designated by the legislature). It's worth noting that there exists a significant disparity in the tax burden, with residential property enjoying preferential treatment. The maximum rates for residential properties are, on average, nearly 30 times lower for buildings and twice as low for land as for business properties. In the case of business activities, preferential rates apply to buildings or their parts used for providing healthcare services, occupied by entities offering such services (approximately 20% of the standard rate), and utilised for business activities in certified seed material trade (approximately 46.5% of the standard rate).

Tax rates are statutorily established and represent only the upper limits for each tax year. Polish municipal councils are obligated to specify these rates in their resolutions. They have the authority to set rates independently, meaning they can either maintain them as prescribed by law or reduce them. Consequently, there are varying taxation levels across different local jurisdictions. Municipal councils are empowered to further categorise taxable objects and their corresponding rates within the statutory framework. The right to differentiate tax rates within individual groups of taxable objects is a critical aspect of local taxing power.

Real estate tax regulations in Poland include specific preferences such as tax exemptions. These exemptions can either entirely or partially relieve certain groups of taxpayers or particular portions of the taxable object from tax obligations. These preferences can be categorised into two groups: (1) object- and subject-based exemptions directly listed in the Act on Local Taxes and Fees and (2) subject-based exemptions introduced by municipal council resolutions. The first object-based group includes exemptions such as farm buildings situated on agricultural land and exclusively used for agricultural activities and non-arable land or railway structures. This group encompasses exemptions granted to entities such as universities, scientific institutes, research institutes, and public and private educational organisations.

Municipalities have considerable flexibility in introducing exemptions within the other group, subject only to adhering to state aid regulations.

Local taxes related to real estate, which constitute municipalities' revenue in Romania, encompass taxes on buildings and land tax, among others (Parlamentul României 2003). The real estate taxation system has evolved significantly over the last quarter of a century. Since 2015, modifications have been made to the taxation system for dwellings, where the annual tax imposed on owners is now determined based on the final use of the property (residential, business, or a combination thereof) rather than the legal status of the owner (individual or company). This implies a standardisation of taxation criteria for previously distinct groups of entities.

In Romania, taxation on residential buildings and annexes owned by individuals is calculated using a rate set annually by municipalities, ranging between 0.08% and 0.2% relative to the established tax value of the building. The tax value of a building is determined by multiplying the built-up area, measured in square metres, by the corresponding tax value per square metre of the area. Two factors influence the tax value of a building's square metre. The first factor is the type of construction of the building and its technical installations. There are six types of building construction identified in legislation, each with statutory tax rates per square metre of the building area, differentiated according to the presence of plumbing, electrical, and heating installations. The municipality's impact primarily lies in the scale of the indexation of the rates per square metre for the various building types. The tax amount is also influenced by the age of the building and discretionary tax preferences that municipalities may apply. These preferences can be related to the nature of the activities conducted by the owner (e.g. social, cultural, and charitable activities), limited owners' income (e.g. allowances), or seasonal use of the property.

The other factor affecting the tax amount is location. The tax rate per square metre is adjusted based on the rank of the locality and the area in which the building is situated. The Romanian legislature permits the introduction of zones (up to four) within individual urban areas of municipalities and specifies six location ranks to differentiate adjustment coefficients. Local authorities have significant discretion in defining these zones. Zone-based multipliers vary from 2.6 in the highest-ranked locality (capital city) and the very centre to 0.9 in the furthest zone of the lowest-ranked locality. For buildings utilised for non-residential purposes by individuals, the rates range from 0.2% to 1.3% of the value of the building (0.4% for buildings used for agricultural activities). The rules for determining the tax value of a building differ from those for residential buildings. An appraisal report is applied, as well as the final value of construction work in the case of new buildings or the value resulting from the ownership transfer document. The tax rates for legal persons are similar to those for individuals. Still, the taxable value of the real estate is calculated either similarly to non-residential buildings of individuals or based on data from tax and accounting records. The property value is updated once every five years.

Similar methodologies apply to land tax. The tax is calculated based on the land area, the rank of the locality (six), the location (zone) within the locality (four), and the land use category (nine) as classified by the local government. In the case of built-up land in urban areas, statutory ranges have been imposed on the fixed amount rates per hectare of land for given categories of locality and zone, which limits local governments' flexibility to enact their tax policies in this area. For instance, the highest (possible) rate in a capital city might be six times the lowest possible rate in that city. However, this rate can be nearly 60 times the maximum rate in the lowest-ranking locality and about 150 times the minimum possible rate in an urban area country-wide. Such disparities imply significant differences in the fiscal capacity of this source of local government revenue, as imposed by the legislature. A similar approach (rank, zone) is applied for other land in urban areas, albeit without rate ranges. Here, the maximum rates per hectare are eight times the minimum rates. Ten land use categories have been established for plots outside urban regions, each with predefined fixed amount ranges for rates per hectare.

In Romanian land taxation, as in building taxation, the catalogue of exemptions and reliefs is divided into a group of exemptions mandated by the statute and another group of reliefs and exemptions at the discretion of municipal authorities.

Since 2005, Slovakia has implemented new regulations on real estate taxation, as provided in the Act on Local Taxes and Local Levy for Municipal Waste and Minor Construction Waste (Národná Rada Slovenskej republiky 2004). Real estate tax in Slovakia consists of land tax, tax on buildings, tax on apartments, and non-residential premises within apartment buildings (in short, apartment tax). It is primarily an area-based tax, except for the land tax, where the value of the land is determined by statute. Municipalities are designated as the administrators of the real estate tax and are its sole beneficiaries.

The subject of land is land in Slovakia, and the taxpayers encompass landowners, administrators (state or municipal land), or, in specific cases as outlined by law, lessees. The tax base is the value of the land without vegetation, determined differently based on the type of land. Each municipality sets the value individually for certain land types (e.g., arable land). In contrast, for others (e.g. gardens, built-up areas, and courtyards), the value depends on the municipality's population and whether the municipality is the seat of a district (*obec*) or region (*kraj*). Separate values have been established for Bratislava. In the case of forest land with forests used for commercial purposes, fish-breeding ponds, and other water bodies used for commercial purposes, the value of the land is determined by the provisions for determining the general property value. The annual rate of land tax is set at 0.25%. Municipalities can increase or reduce this rate within the prescribed limits. Typically, higher land tax rates are established for the city centre in larger cities, while lower rates apply to suburban areas (Vartašová and Červená 2020).

In Slovakia, the taxpayer of the tax on the building is primarily the building owner. However, it can also include the administrator of a state or municipal building, the lessee of buildings administrated by the Slovak Land Fund, or the actual user. Buildings with at least one above-ground or underground storey are subject to taxation, with specific exemptions provided by law. The tax base for buildings is the built-up area in square metres, with a tax rate of EUR 0.033 per m^2 of built-up area or part thereof. Municipalities can increase or reduce this rate, and various tax rates may be set for different types of buildings. The highest rates are typically set for industrial and other business buildings, with consideration also given to locations in larger cities (Vartašová and Červená 2020). Municipalities may implement floor surcharges and apply coefficients to increase the tax rate for unmaintained buildings within specified limits.

The taxpayer of the apartment tax is the owner or administrator – in the case of the premises owned by the state or a local authority. The tax base is the area of the apartment or non-residential premises in square metres. Similar to the tax on buildings, the annual tax rate of apartment tax is EUR 0.033 for each square metre of the area of the apartment or non-residential premises, including incomplete areas. Municipal authorities have the discretion to adjust tax rates based on local circumstances. The rates of this tax vary greatly, with rates for non-residential premises intended for business activities typically several times higher than rates for apartments (Vartašová and Červená 2020).

Numerous statutory exemptions apply to Slovak real estate taxes, and municipalities can introduce additional exemptions or reductions.

Table 3.6 briefly summarises the essential elements of real estate taxation (tax base and tax rates) in the countries discussed above.

3.2.2 Is ad valorem a solution?

The area-based real estate taxation system raises numerous concerns regarding tax justice and equality, rendering the differentiation of tax burdens based on the type and value of real estate assets held by taxpayers unattainable. Similarly, specific tax rate systems fail to consider taxpayers' ability to pay. Owners of properties with lower market values bear the same tax burden as owners of properties with significantly higher values and standards. Area-based taxation schemes for land prove less efficient than value-based schemes, as local authorities have a restricted ability to influence rational transformations in the spatial structure of cities and the efficient utilisation of properties. This is because these schemes foster land holding for speculative purposes, where properties are acquired with a view to their value appreciation. This trend poses a significant challenge, particularly in cities with limited land availability for investment. In such systems, the effectiveness of taxation as a

Table 3.6 The tax base and tax rates in real estate taxes across selected countries of Central and Eastern Europe

Country name	*Tax name*	*Tax base*	*Rates*
Czechia	Land tax	Land area (land value is sometimes taken into account)	In the value-base system for land: 0.45% or 1.35% of the value. In other cases, the basic rate ranges from 0.08 CZK to CZK 9 per 1 m^2.
	Tax on buildings and units	Area of the building or units	The basic rate ranges from CZK 3.5 to CZK 18 per 1 m^2.
Hungary	Land tax	Land area in square metres or adjusted market value	The rate limits are set at HUF 200 per m^2 (increased by the annual cumulative inflation rate) or 3% of the adjusted market value.
	Building tax	Usable area in square metres or adjusted market value	The rate limits are set at HUF 1,100 per m^2 (adjustable by the annual cumulative inflation rate) or 3.6% of the adjusted market value.
Poland	Real estate tax	The tax base is determined by the land area, the usable area of buildings or parts thereof, and the value of structures.	In 2024, the maximum rates for land range from PLN 0.71 to PLN 6.66 per m^2, for buildings or parts thereof from PLN 1.15 per square metre to PLN 33.10, and 2% of the value for structures.
Romania	Tax on buildings	The tax value is determined based on the building's final use, derived from the area and the value of 1 m^2, which is determined by including the installations in one of the groups (adjusted by various indicators).	The tax rate for residential buildings ranges from 0.08% to 0.2% of the tax value, while for non-residential buildings, it ranges from 0.2% to 1.3% of the tax value. The tax rate is set at 0.4% for buildings associated with the agricultural activities of legal persons.
	Land tax	The area in ha depends on the location and category of the locality in which they are situated or how they are used.	The local authority sets the fixed amount-based rate for parts of the sites within statutory ranges.
Slovakia	Land tax	Land statutory value	The basic rate is 0.25%; it may be increased or reduced.
	Tax on buildings	Built-up area in square metres	The annual tax rate is EUR 0.033 per m^2 of built-up area; it may be increased or reduced.
	Apartment tax	The area of an apartment or non-residential premises	The annual tax rate is EUR 0.033 per m^2 of an apartment or non-residential premises; it may be increased or reduced.

Source: Authors' compilation based on legislation governing real estate taxation in selected countries.

tool for shaping efficient spatial policies and fostering local socio-economic development falls short of expectations.

Area-based schemes are typically characterised by their straightforward implementation at the tax stage. Tax collection does not require investment in costly mechanisms for property valuation and indexation of property values. However, this simplicity is often elusive, and accurate tax assessment is challenging. Determining the appropriate tax classification for certain real estate types demands substantial commitment from taxpayers, usually involving financial expenses if tax advisors are engaged. Furthermore, taxpayers with properties across multiple municipalities must consider the possibility of local tax authorities' differential treatment of their assets. The absence of a standardised approach to identical assets complicates taxpayers' tax planning processes and pursued tax strategies.

All the countries that are analysed in Section 3.2.1 employ predominantly area-based real estate taxation systems. In Czechia, the value approach is applied minimally, while in Slovakia, the value approach is used in one of the real estate taxes – the land tax – where the real estate value is determined according to statutory regulations. Although property tax in Hungary can be both value-based and area-based, in practice, most municipalities opt for the area-based approach (Hoffman 2019). One reason for this preference is the difficulty in determining the adjusted fair market value (PwC 2024).

Similarly, in Poland, the real estate taxation system is mixed. The area of the property serves as the tax base for land and buildings, while the value determined by the legislature applies to structures. Although this tax is considered the primary source of municipalities' revenue, structural weaknesses within the real estate taxation system restrict its fiscal capacity. The Polish system is perceived as outdated and not aligned with the solutions adopted by most EU countries (see Etel 2016).

The Romanian real estate taxation system has been assessed as overly complex, lacking transparency, unfair, susceptible to manipulation, and restricting the taxing power of local governments (cf. e.g. Mitu and Mitu 2022). The system's inefficiency has also been highlighted (IMF 2022). Nevertheless, efforts have been made to address these issues by developing solutions to objectively differentiate (qualitatively and quantitatively) the revenue capacity of local governments. This has been achieved by introducing strictly defined rules for determining the ranks of individual units and linking the conversion values of square metres and hectares of area accordingly.

In recent years, there have been numerous debates surrounding changes in real estate taxation, and some of the analysed countries have also tried to implement new solutions, albeit without consistent success.

Given the relatively modest revenue generated by Czech real estate taxes, proposals have emerged to introduce an ad valorem system to augment municipal revenue. However, these proposals, which were to apply to some of the objects subject to land tax, could potentially impose an additional financial burden on municipalities, which might not always be offset by increased tax revenue (Radvan 2019). According to Radvan and Kranecová (2021), the introduction of an ad valorem system is not currently under consideration. This assertion is supported by recent developments primarily centred on changes in tax rates and coefficients affecting the amount of tax liability.

Attempts to reform and strengthen the ad valorem system in Hungary proved unsuccessful. In 2006, a luxury tax was introduced, covering residential properties worth more than HUF 100 million (equivalent to approximately EUR 400,000). The value of real estate was determined based on the "value map", which was attached to the act introducing this tax, and the tax rate was 0.5% of the value of residential buildings above the threshold of HUF 100 million. The method of determining the value of the property raised many objections. In 2008, the act was abolished by the Constitutional Court, which indicated that the statutory provisions were discriminatory and violated the principles of fair and individual treatment (more: Hoffman 2019). In 2010, the Constitutional Court also invalidated another law (from 2009), introducing similar solutions (Hulkó and Feher 2021).

In Poland, the most likely way to improve the current model of real estate taxation is to introduce legal changes aimed at removing the emerging problems in terms of underdeveloped definitions of a structure and a building. In 2023, the Constitutional Tribunal addressed this matter, issuing two judgements declaring specific provisions regarding taxation unconstitutional. The introduction of the indicated changes should provide an impetus for further necessary evolutionary changes.

Romania has witnessed numerous systemic changes over the past two decades. Further reform was planned to enter into force in 2023, which aimed to increase the taxing power of local governments by, among other things, abandoning tax brackets set by law to a minimum rate for buildings and related land. The tax burden was intended to be determined based on the estimated indicative market value per square metre of the building, as determined by the National Association of Notaries. Still, despite the development of the reform assumptions, these changes were not enacted.

Similarly, in Slovakia, there have been discussions over the last decade regarding the reform of real estate taxation towards adopting a value-based approach perceived to be more efficient and fair. However, according to Vartašová (2021), introducing an ad valorem tax in the current conditions would not be advisable. The problem is primarily the insufficient database necessary for the new system's successful introduction and its high costs for updating. There is also no public support for such a reform. Technical obstacles, particularly the lack of price maps providing information on the market price of real estate, are also indicated by the Ministry of Finance (Ministry of Finance of the Slovak Republic 2022).

3.3 How can local authorities influence tax revenue?

The factors influencing the fiscal capacity of property taxation that are within the control of local authorities include primarily the tax policy of municipalities. Such policy is intended to meet social needs in the use of public goods and services and ensure local units' socio-economic development. Various factors determine the implementation of local tax policy (Felis 2015b): external (legal and extra-legal) and internal (municipal capacity, creativity and involvement of local authorities, and social characteristics of residents). The tax policy of local governments depends mainly on the legal regulations adopted in a given country regarding the degree of freedom for local governments to design their tax arrangements. In practice, two main approaches to this issue can be identified. The most common solution is to grant local governments limited taxation power, which amounts to a top-down, statutory introduction of local taxes by central authorities and the indication of selected elements of taxation technique concerning which local governments can make decisions. This method is called a closed-list local tax assessment system (Bordás 2022). On the other hand, it is possible to endow local governments with the competence to shape the indicated elements of tax technique and establish new taxes in the territory of the local government concerned. This method is called an open-list local tax assessment system (Hulkó and Pardavi 2022).

Taxing power is an indicator of the freedom and pursuit of municipal own policy. The use of its prerogatives most often boils down to setting rates within the statutory limits, introducing tax reliefs and exemptions, or applying preferences in the payment of local taxes. In the case of the analysed group of countries (Czechia, Hungary, Poland, Romania, and Slovakia), there is a wide variation in the legislature's approach to the freedom of local governments to influence the level of local taxes (Plaček et al. 2020).

For example, in the case of Czechia, local governments can only influence the level of property taxation by applying local coefficients. In the case of other taxes that partly constitute (share of) local government revenue (e.g. PIT, CIT, and gambling tax), the legislator has not provided for the possibility to influence their volume (Radvan 2020). When analysing the taxing power granted to Slovak local authorities, it should be noted that according to Kubincová (2018), "(t)he Constitution of the Slovak Republic has created a space for the imposition of a certain legal obligation and thus also a tax or fee obligation, not only "by the statute", thus a normative legal act that can only be approved by the National Council of the Slovak Republic as the only legislative body, but also by the normative legislation of the bodies of executive power, as well as municipal authorities". In practice, it means that in terms of determining taxes and fee rates, the rate is, in principle, constituted by the municipality. Specific restrictions can be pointed out here due to statutory regulations (Kubincová 2018) limiting rate increases during a period of regulatory change. Still, in principle, municipalities are free to set their rates. It is noteworthy there is one local tax (of minor importance from the point of view of municipalities as a whole) for which there is a statutory rate – the nuclear facility tax. It is essential, however, that in the case of all other taxes, the level of their rates must consider the realisation by taxation of a legitimate objective with a rational basis. The tax should also not constitute an excessive burden on taxpayers, be proportional in the relationship between the public interest and the legitimate individual interests of taxpayers (groups of taxpayers), and not violate the constitutional principle of equality in differentiating between different groups of taxpayers (Kubincová 2018).

In contrast, in the case of Hungary, the legislator in 2015 introduced a new tax solution – the "settlement tax". The tax can be levied on anything not subject to any other public or local tax (Hulkó and Pardavi 2022). Municipalities have a relatively large margin of discretion in setting such taxes. This is an example of those above open-list local tax assessment systems. In these taxes, municipalities have complete freedom to shape all elements of the tax. At the same time, it should be pointed out that the Hungarian municipalities decided to introduce the local taxes listed in the law on their territory (including the local business tax, tourist tax, land tax, and building tax). In practice, many municipalities opt out of most taxes, the most commonly used being the local business tax (Bordás 2022).

Concerning real estate tax, local authorities enjoy a different extent of taxing power, which includes, among others, the power to determine specific components of tax structure: reduce upper tax rates and differentiate their amounts, apply tax preferences in the form of exemptions, as well as postponements and remissions. An active approach to using local tax policy instruments results, at least in the short term, in reducing tax revenue compared to the amount of potential revenue. However, these activities can effectively increase the municipality's taxation subjects and objects.

In the Western European Union countries, the tax base is generally determined based on the property value, in which the property's location plays an important role (Janoušková and Sobotovičová 2019). The ad valorem system better reflects the principle of tax justice, provided that the tax base for immovable property is determined as accurately as possible, i.e. approaching the market value (Radvan 2011). Such a system is considered more fiscally efficient (provided that real estate value is regularly updated). Still, the taxing power of municipalities varies greatly – in some CEE countries employing ad valorem property taxation, the local government is empowered to set tax rates; in others, tax rates are determined at the central level.

The taxing power may vary even within one type of real estate tax. For example, in Lithuania, in the case of immovable property tax, local governments have no such power (uniform tax rates and thresholds for the entire country) for selected real estate types (e.g. for garden, garage, farm, or greenhouse purposes). In contrast, in the case of other immovable property and land (with regard to land tax), they may independently set rates in the fixed range. The legal provisions list the criteria municipalities can consider when setting rates, but ultimately, the choice of differentiating criteria rests with the municipalities. To illustrate, in Vilnius, 2015, the basic tax rate was 1%. At the same time, a reduced rate (0.7%) was applied for buildings related to meeting public needs (e.g. education, sports, and health) and the maximum rate (3.0%) – for exploited but not completed buildings, abounded, or not attended. Regarding land tax, the rates were set at 0.08% for natural persons and 0.12% for legal persons, while unused land was subject to a maximum rate of 4%. This is a common practice of Lithuanian local governments – land and buildings that are not used, not properly used, or abounded are subject to maximum rates. Since it is not always obvious to consider a building/land as unused/unattended or improperly used, local governments create their own procedures for creating lists of such real estate for tax purposes (Sudavičius and Endrijaitis 2020). Moreover, the Vilnius City Municipality Council determined a taxation threshold (up to ten are) for land belonging to specific categories of taxpayers, e.g. people with reduced work capacity or pensioners (Almy 2015; Mingėlaitė and Birškytė 2021).

Only land is taxable in Estonia, and municipalities may apply a tax rate between 0.1% and 2.5%, but the most commonly used tax rate is 1%. Municipalities can also set varying rates for different value zones, which is not yet often used but sometimes leads to a regressive configuration if high-value areas are assigned to a low-value tax band. In mainly rural communities, agricultural land receives preferential tax treatment on social and economic grounds. Some municipalities allow exemptions for retired individuals on their residential lands (Wenner 2018).

In Latvia, the regular tax rates are universal for all municipalities. Hence, local authorities may apply a special tax rate for buildings that are not well maintained (1.5%) or even 3% for buildings whose construction deadline is overdue (Barvika 2020). One of the most popular instruments used by municipalities was setting different tax rates for an owner's inhabited and uninhabited properties (second homes, summer cottages). Since 2014, municipalities have started to utilise the legislated opportunities to actively apply different tax rates based on the taxpayer's identity (that has a declared address and pays PIT or is an owner of an unoccupied home or summerhouse). In Riga, the tax rate for unoccupied land was 1.5% and considerably higher than 1.5% (in some instances up to seven times higher than before) for a vacant building or apartment (compared to 0.3%–0.6% "regular" rates). This decision had a significant positive effect – the number of Riga residents in 2015–2016 showed an upward trend for the first time in many years. Currently, many municipalities (Riga, Jurmala, counties of Riga agglomeration) use property tax as an instrument to attract residents by offering tax relief (usually 50%) on owner-occupied dwellings (Barvika 2020).

In Slovenia, tax rates were set at the central level, and the local government impacted the real estate valuation. Effectively, in the past, as few municipalities utilised this tax, it represented more of a nuisance tax – it represented a relatively minor source of revenue, mainly because it was a discretionary one. A municipality might decide to implement the tax or not. Many municipalities resign from tax collection due to unreliable property records or the lack of capacity to collect the tax (McCluskey and Bevc 2007). The introduction of the mass valuation system changed this situation, but concurrently, municipalities cannot influence the amount of tax revenue (Ulbl and Smodiš 2019). Compensation for building land use is the only property tax municipal councils can impose. The analysis of variance shows that municipalities use taxing power in this tax, mainly by imposing different tax rates (Brajnik, Prebilic, and Kronegger 2022).

In Bulgaria, since 2008, local governments have been able to independently set tax rates in the range of 1.5%–3% (previously, the rate was uniform for the whole country) (Stoilova 2010) but generally range from 0.01% to 0.15% (BolgariaDom 2024). At the same time, there is no legal possibility of applying differential tax rates to property according to use, location, and improvements – these specific characteristics of the properties are reflected in the process of tax base assessment. Due to the significant tax alleviations, the property tax is not an essential source of municipalities' budgets. The taxpayers pay only 50% of the property tax for their permanent, primary residence. Because 95% of the Bulgarian population lives in such properties, this allowance causes significant losses for the municipal budget (Stoilova 2010). Municipalities use the taxing power by differentiating tax rates. With a location-related property value, differences in tax rates are reflected in the share of property tax in tax revenue (Panteleeva 2019).

In the case of the countries described in Sections 3.1 and 3.2, where real estate taxation is primarily an area-based system, the scope of taxing power is also varied. In Poland, the extent of municipal taxing power is defined by Article 168 of the Polish Constitution, under which they are granted the right to set the amount of local taxes and fees within the statutory specified limits. The most noticeable feature of taxing power is setting tax rates. However, this right does not apply to all local taxes, and when the municipalities can set the rates, this does not occur uniformly (Felis et al. 2023). In real estate tax, reductions in upper tax rates are of the most significant importance (in the years 2007–2021, they accounted for, on average, over 68% of all tax expenditure), and tax exemptions are also quite frequently applied (on average, approx. 23%). Individual support instruments, such as remission of tax arrears and payment of tax in instalments, were used to a much smaller extent (9% of all tax expenditure).

It should be noted that the applied preferences change over time, and significant differences between different types of Polish local units are also visible. According to Felis et al.'s research (2023), in the years 2007–2021, due to the reduction in the upper real estate rates, municipalities lost a total of PLN 31.5 billion. This represented a loss of 8.4%–13.5% of annual revenue from this source (11.3% on average over the entire period). In recent years, a significant decline in the use scale of this tax policy instrument has been observed. In 2007–2015, the reduction in tax rates resulted in a fiscal effect of an average of 12.5% of real estate tax revenue, and in 2016–2021, only about 9.4%. This had the most significant impact on the revenue of rural and urban-rural municipalities. The fiscal effects of reducing the upper tax rates in these units amounted, on average, to 19% and approximately 17% of real estate tax revenue, respectively. In urban municipalities – primarily in cities with county rights – the effects of the taxing power were of little significance (less than 4% on average). Therefore, there is a specific relationship (an inverse relationship) between the tax capacity of municipalities (residential, commercial, and industrial base) and the scale of application of tax policy instruments. The effects of municipalities' taxing power also varied depending on the category of taxpayer. Municipalities used their administrative prerogatives much more intensively in relation to real estate owned by natural persons. Revenue was reduced on average by approximately 25%, while for real estate owned by legal persons, this indicator amounted to only approximately 7.5%.

In Romania, the real estate tax has changed considerably over the previous 20 years, for example, as regards the way rates were determined (from statutory imposed rates to rates set at the complete discretion of local governments), taking into account the degree of depreciation of buildings and using elevated tax rates when a taxpayer owns more than one residential premises. The taxing power of Romanian municipalities entails the partial possibility of setting the tax rate (within statutory limits), choosing the base value (likewise), using statutory enumerated exemptions, and, indirectly, delimiting tax zones in the municipality. The local government can also index the base tax amount using the inflation rate. Municipal authorities may also introduce specific tax rate increases in statutory enumerated circumstances.

In Hungary, real estate taxes are administered by municipalities, which act as tax authorities in matters of local taxes. The decision to introduce the tax rests with the municipal authorities, and the municipalities also decide what to choose as the tax base – area in square metres (land or usable area) or adjusted market value. Even though few municipalities have decided to introduce a real estate tax, it is a relatively important source of local revenue.

Slovak municipalities may vary land tax rates within their territory. In larger cities, the rates are usually higher for the central districts and lower for the suburbia. In the case of tax on buildings, the highest rates are almost always set for industrial buildings and other business sites. At the same time, the location (distance from the city centre) is also considered in larger cities. Apartment tax rates vary primarily because of the nature of the premises. The real estate tax rates currently in force are almost three times higher than the time the tax was introduced, and the highest growth took place in 2004–2005 when local government authorities began to exercise the granted taxing power (Vartašová and Červená 2020).

Although the real estate tax in Czechia is a municipal tax, until 2009, the taxing power of municipalities concerning this tax was severely limited. At that time, they could only make minor adjustments to tax rates. In 2009, a local coefficient was introduced (with a value of 2, 3, 4, or 5), and municipalities could adopt only one value for all properties in their area. According to Ministry of Finance estimates, thanks to this coefficient, the municipalities can increase their revenue by as much as 10% (Sedmihradská 2013). However, the newly introduced solution was not widely used. Studies by Formanová, Halamová, and Andrlík (2020) on the low use of the local coefficient suggested that the main reason was the reluctance of citizens to increase the tax burden and the view that the introduction of the coefficient would affect the ratings of municipal authorities. Many municipalities do not apply the local coefficient due to the meagre share of receipts from this tax in the total revenue structure. It has been noticed that municipalities introducing a local coefficient often waive local fees, primarily the fee for municipal waste. Municipalities do not bear the costs of collecting the real estate tax – central units administer it. Additional tax revenue allows you to finance expenses previously covered by fees, the collection of which is funded through the municipal budget. In 2019, the coefficient was used by approximately 10% of municipalities. Municipalities' interest in introducing a local coefficient may be encouraged by the changes introduced in 2021. Since then, the coefficient can vary between different parts of the municipality and may be set to any value from a set range and not as before – from four designated values. In 2024, the scope of land for which municipalities can introduce a local coefficient was extended, and the ranges of values in which this coefficient may be included were changed.

According to the theory of fiscal federalism, decentralised territorial communities should be characterised by a specific scope of local tax autonomy, and taxing power should be perceived as an essential determinant of local financial autonomy. In the countries of Central and Eastern Europe presented in this chapter, the freedom and opportunities to create one's tax policy are relatively small. Despite the limitations mentioned above, municipalities can influence the amount of real estate tax revenue. However, the activity of local authorities in this area is limited for various reasons. Decisions made in this area may lead to an increase in revenue and a reduction in the short term, which would not be a desirable and rational action in a time of permanent income shortages. The share of real estate taxes in municipal budgets is also essential – in most analysed countries, their fiscal importance is insignificant. One cannot ignore issues related to the overall systemic regulation of municipalities' financial management, including solutions aimed at fiscal equalisation.

Bibliography

Almy, Richard. 2015. "Property Valuation and Taxation for Improving Local Governance in Europe and Central Asia: Lithuania Case Study." In *Turto vertinimo teorijos ir praktikos apybraižos 2014–2015*, edited by Steponas Deveikis, 6–29. Vilnius: Lietuvos turto vertintojų asociacija.

Bahl, Roy W. 1999. "Implementation Rules for Fiscal Decentralization." In *International Studies Program Working Paper Series 99-01, Andrew Young School of Policy Studies*. Georgia State University.

Barvika, Sarmite. 2020. *The Property Tax in Latvia: System Structure and Current Challenges*. Cambridge, MA: Lincoln Institute of Land Policy.

Baskaran, Thushyanthan, and Lars P. Feld. 2013. "Fiscal Decentralization and Economic Growth in OECD Countries: Is There a Relationship?" *Public Finance Review* 41 (4): 421–445.

Blöchliger, Hansjorg, and Oliver Petzold. 2009. "Finding the Dividing Line Between Tax Sharing and Grants: A Statistical Investigation." *OECD Working Papers on Fiscal Federalism*, no. 10. Paris: OECD Publishing. doi:10.1787/5k97b10vvbnw-en.

BolgariaDom. 2024. "Taxes and Fees When Buying Real Estate in Bulgaria in 2024." https://bolgariadom.com/en/taxes-and-fees-when-buying-real-estate-in-bulgaria-in-2024.

Bordás, Peter. 2022. "Experiences Od Open and Closed List Local Taxes in Hungary with Special Regard to the Effects of the COVID-19 Pandemic." *Review of European and Comparative Law* 50 (3): 181–199. doi:10.31743/recl.13507.

Brajnik, Irena Bačlija, Vladimir Prebilic, and Luka Kronegger. 2022. "Explaining Strategies in Setting Own Local Taxes in Slovenia." *Lex Localis: Journal of Local Self-Government* 20 (1): 239–257. doi:10.4335/20.1.239-257(2022).

Česká Národní Rada. 1992. *Zákon České Národní Rady o Dani z Nemovitých Věcí. 338.* https://www.zakonyprolidi.cz/cs/1992-338/zneni-20240101.

CSO. 2023. "Economy of Regions and Municipalities." *Czech Statistical Office - Public Database.* https://vdb.czso.cz/vdbvo2/faces/en/index.jsf?page=statistiky&katalog=33877.

Dougherty, Sean, Michelle Harding, and Andrew Reschovsky. 2019. "Twenty Years of Tax Autonomy across Levels of Government: Measurement and Applications." *OECD Working Papers on Fiscal Federalism* 29 (December). doi:10.1787/ca7ebc02-en.

Etel, Leonard. 2016. "Opodatkowanie nieruchomości – kierunki pożądanych zmian, w: Dylematy reformy systemu podatkowego w Polsce." In *Dylematy reformy systemu podatkowego w Polsce*, edited by Henryk Dzwonkowski and Jacek Kulicki, 414–435. Biblioteka Analiz Sejmowych. Warszawa: Wydawnictwo Sejmowe.

European Charter of Local Self-Government. 1985. Strasbourg. https://www.congress-monitoring.eu/.

European Commission. 2022. *2022 Country Report – Romania*. SWD/2022/624 final. Brussels: European Commission. https://publications.europa.eu/resource/comnat/SWD_2022_0624_FIN.

European Commission. 2023. "Data on Taxation Trends." *Taxation and Customs Union.* https://taxation-customs.ec.europa.eu/taxation-1/economic-analysis-taxation/data-taxation-trends_en.

Felis, Paweł. 2012. *Elementy teorii i praktyki podatków majątkowych: poszukiwanie ładu w opodatkowaniu nieruchomości w Polsce z perspektywy przedsiębiorców oraz jednostek samorządu terytorialnego*. Monografie i Opracowania / Szkoła Główna Handlowa 588. Warszawa: Oficyna Wydawnicza SGH - Szkoła Główna Handlowa.

Felis, Paweł. 2015a. "Funkcja Fiskalna i Społeczna w Powierzchniowym Systemie Opodatkowania Nieruchomości Na Przykładzie Gmin w Polsce." *Gospodarka Narodowa. The Polish Journal of Economics* 277 (3): 133–158. doi:10.33119/GN/100841.

Felis, Paweł. 2015b. *Podatki od nieruchomości a polityka podatkowa gmin w Polsce*. Warszawa: Oficyna Wydaw. Szkoła Główna Handlowa.

Felis, Paweł, Leszek Patrzałek, Angieszka Bem, Michał Bernardelli, Elżbieta Malinowska-Misiąg, Jarosław Olejniczak, and Milena Kowalska. 2023. *Opodatkowanie nieruchomości w Polsce na tle wybranych państw Europy Środkowo-Wschodniej : koncepcje przekształceń*. 1st ed. Wroclaw: Wroclaw University of Economics and Business. doi:10.15611/2023.44.2.

Formanová, Lucie, Martina Halamová, and Břetislav Andrlík. 2020. "Utilization of a Local Coefficient for Immovable Property Tax in the Czech Republic." *Acta Universitatis Agriculturae et Silviculturae Mendelianae Brunensis* 68 (6): 973–986. doi:10.11118/actaun202068060973.

Hoffman, Istvan. 2019. "Jedynie teoretyczna możliwość wprowadzenia katastralnego systemu opodatkowania nieruchomości – uregulowania w zakresie podatków od nieruchomości na Węgrzech." *Analizy i Studia CASP* 8 (2): 71–83. doi:10.33119/ASCASP.2019.2.5.

Hulkó, Gábor, and Julia Feher. 2021. "Hungary." In *Real Property Taxes and Property Markets in CEE Countries and Central Asia*, edited by Michal Radvan, Riel Franzsen, William McCluskey, and Franzes Plimmer, 143–177. Maribor: Lex Localis - Institute for Local Self-Government.

Hulkó, Gábor, and László Pardavi. 2022. "Practical Experience and the Significance of the Settlement Tax in Hungary." *Annual Center Review* 14–15: 43–49. https://doi.org/10.15290/acr.2021-2022.14-15.06.

Hungarian Central Statistical Office. 2024a. "Detailed List of Taxes and Social Contributions According to National Classification – Local Government." *Hungarian Central Statistical Office*. https://www.ksh.hu/stadat_files/gdp/en/gdp0028.html.

Hungarian Central Statistical Office. 2024b. "Main Aggregates of General Government." *Hungarian Central Statistical Office*. https://www.ksh.hu/stadat_files/gdp/en/gdp0017.html.

IMF. 2022. *Romania Technical Assistance Report on Improving Revenues from The Recurrent Property Tax*. Washington, DC: IMF.

Janoušková, Jana, and Šárka Sobotovičová. 2019. "Fiscal Autonomy of Municipalities in the Context of Land Taxation in the Czech Republic." *Land Use Policy* 82 (March): 30–36. doi:10.1016/j.landusepol.2018.11.048.

Kubincová, Soňa. 2018. "Local Taxes and Fees in the Slovak Republic in the Context of the European Charter of Local Self-Government." *Scientific Journal of Bielsko-Biala School of Finance and Law* 22 (1): 32–37. doi:10.19192/wsfip.sj1.2018.5.

Leodolter, Alexander, Savina Princen, and Alexander Rutkowski. 2022. *Immovable Property Taxation for Sustainable & Inclusive Growth*. European Economy - Discussion Papers 156. Luxembourg: Publications Office of the European Union.

Mauro, Luciano, Francesco Pigliaru, and Gaetano Carmeci. 2018. "Decentralization and Growth: Do Informal Institutions and Rule of Law Matter?" *Journal of Policy Modeling* 40 (5): 873–902. doi:10.1016/j.jpolmod.2018.05.003.

McCluskey, William J., and Igor Bevc. 2007. "Fiscal Decentralization in the Republic of Slovenia: An Opportunity for the Property Tax." *Property Management* 25 (4): 400–419. doi:10.1108/02637470710775220.

MFSR. 2024. "Územná Samospráva." *Ministerstvo Financií Slovenskej Republiky*. https://www.mfsr.sk/sk/financie/verejne-financie/uzemna-samosprava.

Mingėlaitė, Dovile, and Liucija Birškytė. 2021. "Broad-Based Low-Rate Property Tax in Lithuania." In *Real Property Taxes and Property Markets in CEE Countries and Central Asia*, edited by Michal Radvan, Riel Franzsen, William McCluskey, and Franzes Plimmer, 177–217. Maribor: Lex Localis Press.

Ministerstwo Finansów. 2023. "Sprawozdania Budżetowe." *Sprawozdania Budżetowe*. https://www.gov.pl/web/finanse/sprawozdania-budzetowe.

Ministry of Finance of the Slovak Republic. 2022. "Stability Programme of the Slovak Republic for 2022 to 2025." https://commission.europa.eu/system/files/2022-06/2022-slovakia-stability-programme_en.pdf.

Mitu, Narcis, and George Mitu. 2022. "Reforming the Property Tax System in Romania: A Necessity." *Revista de Stiinte Politice. Revue des Sciences Politiques* April: 99–113.

Národná Rada Slovenskej republiky. 2004. Zákon o Miestnych Daniach a Miestnom Poplatku Za Komunálne Odpady a Drobné Stavebné Odpady. 582. https://www.zakonypreludi.sk/zz/2004-582.

Országgyűlés. 1990. *1990. Évi C. Törvény a Helyi Adókról. 138*. https://njt.hu/eli/TV/1990/100.

Pahl, Bogumił. 2009. "Podstawa opodatkowania w podatku od nieruchomości – problemy praktyczne." *Studia Ełckie* 11 (1): 247–261.

Panteleeva, V. 2019. "Local Taxes in Bulgaria-a Source of Revenues in the Municipality Budgets." *Challenges of the Knowledge Society* 13 (1): 725–731.

Parlamentul României. 2003. *Codul Fiscal. 571*. https://legislatie.just.ro/Public/DetaliiDocument/48725.

Pest, Przemysław. 2014. "Wysokość udziałów jednostek samorządu terytorialnego we wpływach z podatków dochodowych." *Acta Universitatis Wratislaviensis* 3608: 117–127.

Plaček, Michal, František Ochrana, Milan Jan Půček, and Juraj Nemec. 2020. "The Fiscal Decentralization in Romania." In *Fiscal Decentralization Reforms: The Impact on the Efficiency of Local Governments in Central and Eastern Europe*, edited by Michal Plaček, František Ochrana, Milan Jan Půček, and Juraj Nemec, 93–100. Cham: Springer International Publishing. doi:10.1007/978-3-030-46758-6_6.

PwC. 2024. "Hungary. Building and Land Taxes." https://taxsummaries.pwc.com/hungary/corporate/other-taxes.

Radvan, Michal. 2011. "Negativa zdanění nemovitostí ad valorem." In *Dny práva 2011 – Days of Law 2011. Finance veřejného sektoru (právní a ekonomické aspekty jeho fungování)*, edited by David Sehnálek, 319–327. Brno: Days of Law.

Radvan, Michal. 2019. "Główne zagadnienia problematyczne związane z opodatkowaniem nieruchomości w Republice Czeskiej." *Analizy i Studia CASP* 8 (2): 15–35.

Radvan, Michal. 2020. *Czech Tax Law*. Brno: Masaryk University.

Radvan, Michal, and Jana Czudek Kranecová. 2021. "Is Ad Valorem Property Taxation a Solution for the Czech Republic." In *Real Property Taxes and Property Markets in CEE Countries and Central Asia*, edited by Michal Radvan, Riel Franzsen, William McCluskey, and Franzes Plimmer, 47–78. Maribor: Lex Localis - Institute for Local Self-Government.

Ricciuti, Roberto, Antonio Savoia, and Kunal Sen. 2019. "How Do Political Institutions Affect Fiscal Capacity? Explaining Taxation in Developing Economies." *Journal of Institutional Economics* 15 (2): 351–380. doi:10.1017/S1744137418000097.

Sedmihradská, Lucie. 2013. "Yardstick Competition in Case of the Czech Property Tax." *Review of Economic Perspectives – Národohospodářský Obzor* 13 (2): 77–91. doi:10.2478/revecp-2013-0002.

Sejm Rzeczpospolitej Polskiej. 1991. *Ustawa z 12 Stycznia 1991 r. o Podatkach i Opłatach Lokalnych. 31.* Vol. 9. https://isap.sejm.gov.pl/isap.nsf/DocDetails.xsp?id=WDU19910090031.

Shah, Anwar. 1994. *The Reform of Intergovernmental Fiscal Relations in Developing and Emerging Market Economies*. Vol. 23. Policy & Research Series. Washington, D.C.: The World Bank.

Spatari, Marcel. 2020. *The Inequity of the Fiscal System in Romania. The Case of Property Tax*. Romania: Friedrich-Ebert-Stiftung.

Stibůrková, Ivana, Tomas Havel, and Mirka Malá. 2023. "Consolidation Package I: Overview of Main Changes in Taxation." KPMG. https://danovky.cz/en/news/detail/1219.

Stoilova, Desislava. 2010. "Property Tax in Bulgaria: A Case Study of Blagoevgrad." In *Property Tax in Economies in Transition: Selected Case Studies*, edited by Lucie Sedmihradská, 30–56. Bratislava: NISPAcee Press.

Sudavičius, Bronius, and Martynas Endrijaitis. 2020. "Increased Tax Rates in the Taxation System of the Republic of Lithuania." *Правоприменение* 4 (2): 28–40. doi:10.24147/2542-1514.2020.4(2).28-40.

Thornton, John. 2007. "Fiscal Decentralization and Economic Growth Reconsidered." *Journal of Urban Economics* 61 (1): 64–70. doi:10.1016/j.jue.2006.06.001.

Ulbl, Melita, and Martin Smodiš. 2019. "Prenova sistema množičnega vrednotenja nepremičnin v Sloveniji." *Geodetski Vestnik* 63 (3): 325–343. doi:10.15292/geodetski-vestnik.2019.03.325-343.

Vartašová, Anna. 2021. "Adequacy of Current System of Property Taxation in the Slovak Republic." In *Real Property Taxes and Property Markets in CEE Countries and Central Asia*, edited by Michal Radvan, Riel Franzsen, William J. McCluskey, and Franzes Plimmer, 80–117. Maribor: Lex Localis - Institute for Local Self-Government.

Vartašová, Anna, and Karolina Červená. 2020. "Podatki lokalne – źródło finansowania samorządu lokalnego na Słowacji." In *Regulacje prawa finansów publicznych i prawa podatkowego: podsumowanie stanu obecnego i dynamika zmian*, edited by Paweł Borszowski, Katarzyna Kopyściańska, Marek Kopyściański, Witold Srokosz and Patrycja Zawadzka, 664–675. Warszawa: Wolters Kluwer.

Wenner, Fabian. 2018. "Sustainable Urban Development and Land Value Taxation: The Case of Estonia." *Land Use Policy* 77: 790–800. doi:10.1016/j.landusepol.2016.08.031.

4 Motives of municipal tax policy

4.1 Methodology and scope of the analysis

This chapter uses data gathered based on the following:

1 a focus study with the participation of commune heads;
2 a questionnaire conducted on a resident sample;
3 a questionnaire conducted on a municipality sample;
4 a tax return on the real estate tax, agricultural tax, and forest tax (further: SP-1 Tax Return).

The focus study took place on 5 May 2022. A focus group worked remotely via MS Teams for 1 hour and 35 minutes. With the participants' consent, the meeting was recorded and then transcribed. Eight people participated in the study: two representatives of a rural municipality, two of an urban municipality, two of an urban-rural municipality, and representatives of cities with county rights. The group was homogenous and consisted of executive representatives (commune heads) appointed through direct elections. Two facilitators/scenario authors took part in the study.

The participants had already read the study scenario. The questions asked in the scenario referred to the following study questions formulated based on a review of literature presented in the first chapter of the monograph:

1 Do the municipalities experience local tax competition or apply a competition policy for the tax base? (*local tax competition*);
2 Do local politicians make decisions based on the views of the residents? (*average voter model*);
3 Do the authorities pursue a different local tax policy in the election years than during other stages of their term of office? (*political business cycle*);
4 Is the local tax policy primarily determined by the ideology of politicians depending on the political party they represent? (*partisan political model*).

The questionnaire survey among residents of municipalities was performed in February 2022 by Biostat. The questionnaire survey covered a sample of

DOI: 10.4324/9781003530503-5

1,000 adult Poles, participants of the Due Diligence Opinion online panel. The sample considered the representative distribution by age and gender compared to the online user population of the analysed age.

The survey tool (questionnaire survey) consisted of personal data (age, gender, education, income, and prevailing source of income), and ten survey questions aimed at determining the perception of the income tax in the context of income burdens, tax justice, and the impact of tax rates on electoral decisions (see the Annex).

For the survey, a questionnaire was also addressed to the municipalities (see the Annex) to verify:

- How do the municipalities view real estate tax?
- What the municipalities are guided by in their tax policy concerning real estate tax?
- What is the municipalities' view on potential real estate tax structure changes?

The survey consisted of 21 questions, and the first introductory question evaluated the municipalities' general level of self-reliance regarding tax-related powers (understood as the right of municipalities to change real estate tax rates and use tax preferences).

Further questions addressed the real estate tax rate depending on the taxpayer category (questions 2 and 3) and the opinion about differentiating tax rates depending on the taxpayer category and selected objects of taxation (question 4). Questions 5–7 were about the criteria for differentiation of tax rates charged on land, buildings, and structures.

The municipalities were also asked to evaluate the impact of various premises on the application of tax preferences in real estate tax (question 8), the impact of rates applied by local municipalities on the amount of own tax rates (question 9), and the level of implementation of goals that justify the shape of tax resolutions (question 10).

Question 11 was about the issues related to the discussion on draft resolutions on the real estate tax, while the next question was about the rights of municipalities related to that tax (question 12). A question was also asked about motions filed by councillor clubs to change real estate tax rates (question 13) and the tax collection issue depending on the taxpayer category (question 14). Question 15 asked about their opinion on the impact of the electoral cycle on unpopular decisions regarding real estate tax rates made by municipality councils.

The final part of the survey (questions 16–21) focused on potential changes to the real estate tax and the perception of the cadastral tax formula.

Five pollsters conducted the questionnaire survey dedicated to municipalities between 10 December 2021 and 18 February 2022. It was addressed to municipalities from five voivodeships with various social and economic profiles: Dolnośląskie, Lubelskie, Mazowieckie, Podlaskie, Śląskie, and Wielkopolskie.

Out of 1,204 surveys, 840 responses were received, accounting for nearly 70% of all the surveys sent out. The highest number of filled-in surveys was recorded for the Śląskie Voivodeship (79%), while the authorities from the Dolnośląskie Voivodeship were the least engaged (59%). Considering the total number of surveys, the highest number of responses came from the Mazowieckie Voivodeship (217) and the lowest from the Podlaskie Voivodeship (82).

Analysis of the return rate by local government authorities showed that cities with county rights were most eager to participate in the survey, with 82% of the surveyed authorities returning the survey, giving a total of 32. The lowest return rate was recorded for urban municipalities (65% or 87 responses). The highest number of surveys was received from rural municipalities (529), with a return rate of 70%.

The financial data (SP-1 Tax Return) come from the Ministry of Finance databases and contain detailed information about local government authorities' revenue, expenditures, liabilities, and receivables.

The Spearman rank correlation was selected for the analysis of correlation obtained in the study of tax competition and the impact of the reduction in upper tax rates on municipality revenue. It is one of the fundamental non-parametric measures of monotone statistical dependence among random variables. Unlike Pearson's linear correlation, Spearman's rank correlation does not require meeting assumptions about the linearity or probability distribution of the random variables analysed. It is also resistant to outliers.

Spearman's rank correlation takes values in the range of −1 to 1, indicating the existence of any monotone dependence, including a non-linear dependence. It differs from the Pearson correlation coefficient in this respect, measuring the linear dependence between two variables. A strict linear dependence or even dependence close to the linear dependence between reductions in the upper tax rates and the municipality revenue is rather unlikely. However, there is a greater chance of interdependence between these variables, which changes over time non-linearly. Moreover, to prove the existence of the studied effect (not its strength), the determined value of Spearman's ρ rank correlation coefficient should be statistically significant. The test of significance for Spearman's rank-order correlation coefficient was used to check the statistical significance with a significance level of 0.05.

4.2 The impact of using tools of tax-related authority on budget revenue – fiscal motive

The definition of the dependence between decisions made and real income is a significant aspect of municipal taxes, and this section describes the impact of reductions in upper tax rates of the real estate tax on municipalities' own revenue and the revenue from real estate tax from 2007 to 2021.

To verify the impact of reductions in upper tax rates on the revenue of Polish municipalities in the subsequent year, an analysis based on Spearman's rank correlation was conducted, which is an adequate measure for verifying the research hypothesis, where in theory, the analysis can account for more considerable delays, which would not change the fact of existence of the studied effect but merely affect its size. The simplification, which consisted of adopting a one-year delay, was primarily dictated by the short duration of the study period, from 2007 to 2021.

The exploration of data on reductions in upper tax rates and municipalities' revenue resulted in several conclusions. Firstly, the mean values of reductions in upper tax rates and municipalities' own revenue have been growing regularly. This observation should be evident if we look at the increase in statutory upper tax rates and the dynamic growth of the real estate market in Poland from the perspective of an increase in statutory upper tax rates. Secondly, standard deviations point to a high diversification of the municipalities, which is much less prevalent if we limit the study to a specific type of municipality. Rural municipalities, urban-rural municipalities, and urban municipalities seem to be more homogenous than cities with county rights when it comes to reductions in upper tax rates, as well as own revenue. High differentiation among individual municipalities is visible, especially regarding the revenue of cities with county rights. Thirdly, the average own revenue and reductions in upper tax rates grow in a monotone manner, along with the increase in the "urban element" in the type of the municipality, namely they are the lowest for rural municipalities, followed by urban-rural municipalities and urban municipalities, and the highest for cities with county rights.

From 2009 to 2021, the average amount of municipalities' own revenue increased year-on-year (see Figure 4.1), which was not linear but strictly

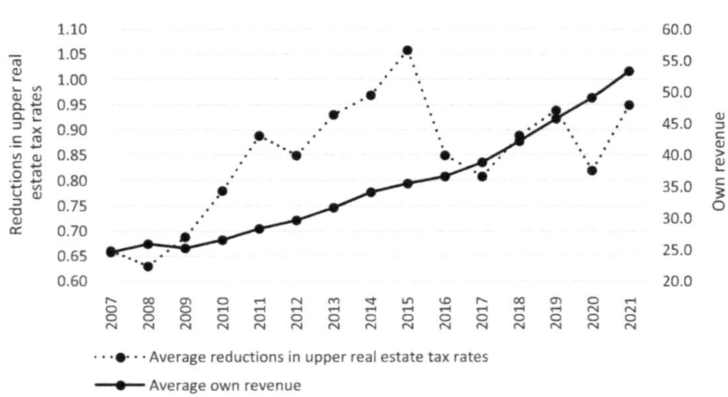

Figure 4.1 Average reductions in upper real estate tax rates (in million PLN) and average municipalities' own revenue (in million PLN) from 2007 to 2021.

Source: Own study.

monotone. The situation is different regarding average (on a national scale) reductions in upper tax rates. While we can speak about a growing trend, there have been years with an apparent decrease in the presence of the dependence among such variables, which is not evident and requires statistical methods.

The analysis was divided into two stages. In the first stage, Spearman's rank correlation was calculated for the following pairs of variables:

reduction – reduction in upper real estate tax rates in a year i,
$revenue_{i+1}$ – municipalities' own revenue in year i+1,

where i = 2007, 2008, …, 2020.

Calculations were performed for all the municipalities, and there was a division into types of municipalities. The values of Spearman's rank correlation coefficient ρ are collated in Table 4.1. All coefficients proved statistically significant at the adopted significance level, with coefficient values ranging from 0.43 to 0.74. However, for the entire population of municipalities (the "Poland" column), the values are pretty stable over time, ranging from 0.61 to 0.74, where lower values can be observed during crisis periods from the viewpoint of the economy, namely the years 2008–2009, 2012–2014, and during the pandemic from 2020 to 2021.

The strength of correlation for various types of municipalities is presented in Figure 4.2. There are evident differences among various types of municipalities, with the lowest correlation recorded for cities with county rights. Over 13 years, the values of Spearman's rank correlation coefficient ρ fell by nearly 25% from 0.56 to as low as 0.43. Moreover, the differences among

Table 4.1 Spearman's rank correlation coefficient ρ between variables $reduction_i$ and $revenue_{i+1}$ for i = 2007, 2008, …, 2020 with a breakdown by municipality type

Year	*Poland*	*Rural municipalities (RM)*	*Urban-rural municipalities (URM)*	*Urban municipalities (UM)*	*Cities with county rights (CCR)*
2007	0.74	0.61	0.66	0.67	0.56
2008	0.62	0.48	0.57	0.64	0.56
2009	0.64	0.51	0.58	0.65	0.50
2010	0.74	0.63	0.65	0.67	0.49
2011	0.73	0.62	0.65	0.68	0.58
2012	0.61	0.49	0.58	0.66	0.48
2013	0.61	0.49	0.60	0.64	0.45
2014	0.62	0.51	0.59	0.63	0.51
2015	0.66	0.55	0.63	0.62	0.55
2016	0.67	0.58	0.63	0.60	0.51
2017	0.67	0.59	0.62	0.60	0.51
2018	0.70	0.62	0.67	0.62	0.56
2019	0.70	0.62	0.66	0.65	0.50
2020	0.64	0.56	0.60	0.57	0.43

Source: Own study.

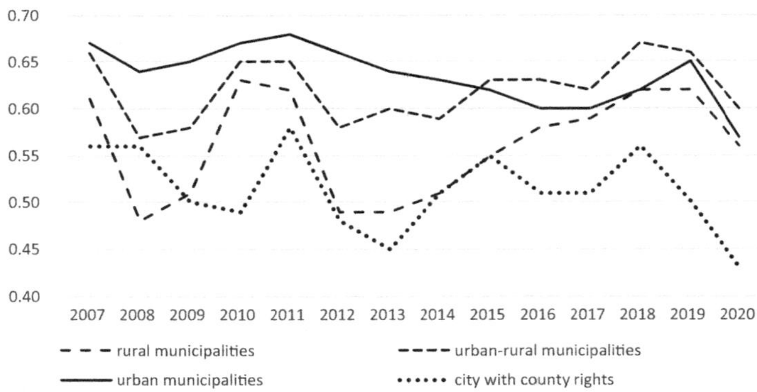

Figure 4.2 List of Spearman's rank correlation coefficient ρ between variables $reduction_i$ and $revenue_{i+1}$ for i = 2007, 2008, …, 2020 with a breakdown by municipality type.

Source: Own study.

other types of municipalities increased, with the convergence phenomenon noticeable over the past years. The economic downturn's consequences seem to mainly affect cities with county rights, while change fluctuations over the last decade were lower for the remaining types of municipalities.

The approach applied at the first stage of analyses can be sectoral, based on data from all the municipalities from a selected year. A shortcoming of such an approach is that the specific nature of a municipality over the years is not accounted for, and it can be easily imagined that an increase in a municipality's revenue can occur but is not related to a reduction in upper tax rates. Thus, capturing a stable relation among the analysed variables is essential over time. Such needs are addressed by the second stage of the analyses, which investigates the existence of correlations for each of nearly 2,500 municipalities separately, which is an example of analysis of time intervals, as individual authorities were studied over the timeframe of 2007–2021. The first stage of the analysis demonstrates correlations for the sectoral view of all municipalities (with municipalities broken down by type if necessary). This does not mean that such dependence will be valid for each municipality, as although some municipalities apply reductions to a minimum extent, there are also municipalities that apply reductions that are too drastic to increase their own revenue. Some municipalities do not pursue a consistent policy in this regard, as well as municipalities whose revenue is affected by other factors, such as external factors related, for example, to tax competition (described in Section 4.3).

As expected, the correlation coefficient values range from −0.96, a significantly negative correlation, to +0.99, a virtually ideal positive correlation.

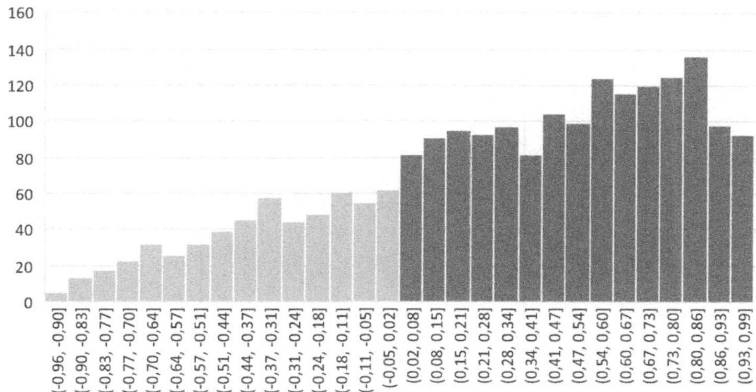

Figure 4.3 A histogram of Spearman's rank correlation coefficient values ρ for the complete set of municipalities. Positive coefficients are marked with a darker colour, while negative coefficients are marked with a lighter colour.

Source: Own study.

The histogram in Figure 4.3 clearly shows that there are considerably more municipalities with a positive Spearman's rank correlation coefficient ρ between the reduction in upper real estate tax rates and municipalities' own revenue.

The value of the correlation coefficient should not be interpreted without running a statistical test to verify its statistical significance. By rejecting statistically insignificant coefficients (significance of 0.05), the distribution of values of Spearman's rank correlation coefficient ρ changes dramatically, with only coefficients higher than or equal to the absolute value of 0.54 proving to be statistically significant. However, the set of negative correlations is still smaller than the set of municipalities with positive coefficients (169 vs 908 municipalities). The quantitative descriptions of both sets are collated in Table 4.2.

The percentage of municipalities with Spearman's rank correlation coefficients ρ that are statistically significant and negative is merely 6.6% of all municipalities. A statistically significant positive correlation was observed for more than one-third of cases. Looking at the types of municipalities, the coefficients are distributed in quite a similar way, and only the median of positive correlation results for cities with county rights (ρ = 0.82) and urban municipalities (ρ = 0.80) is more significant than for other types of municipalities (0.73–0.75). It is also worth stressing that the correlation coefficient determined for nearly 17% of cities with county rights proved to be negative, while for other types of municipalities, the percentage of observed negative correlations ranged from 5% to 12%.

Table 4.2 Descriptive statistics for statistically significant Spearman's rank correlation coefficients ρ between the reduction in upper real estate tax rates and municipalities' own revenue, broken down by the type of municipality

		Number	*Percentage*	*Minimum*	*First quartile*	*Median*	*Mean*	*Third quartile*	*Maximum*
Negative values ρ	POLAND	169	6.60	−0.96	−0.77	−0.68	−0.69	−0.60	−0.54
	RM	78	4.90	−0.96	−0.77	−0.68	−0.69	−0.60	−0.54
	URM	51	7.80	−0.89	−0.78	−0.64	−0.68	−0.59	−0.54
	UM	29	12.00	−0.94	−0.8	−0.71	−0.72	−0.63	−0.54
	CCR	11	16.70	−0.85	−0.74	−0.67	−0.67	−0.61	−0.56
Positive values ρ	POLAND	908	35.60	0.54	0.65	0.75	0.75	0.86	0.99
	RM	600	37.80	0.54	0.65	0.75	0.75	0.85	0.99
	URM	203	31.10	0.54	0.63	0.73	0.74	0.83	0.99
	UM	83	34.30	0.54	0.70	0.80	0.79	0.88	0.98
	CCR	22	33.30	0.56	0.72	0.82	0.80	0.92	0.99

Source: Own study.

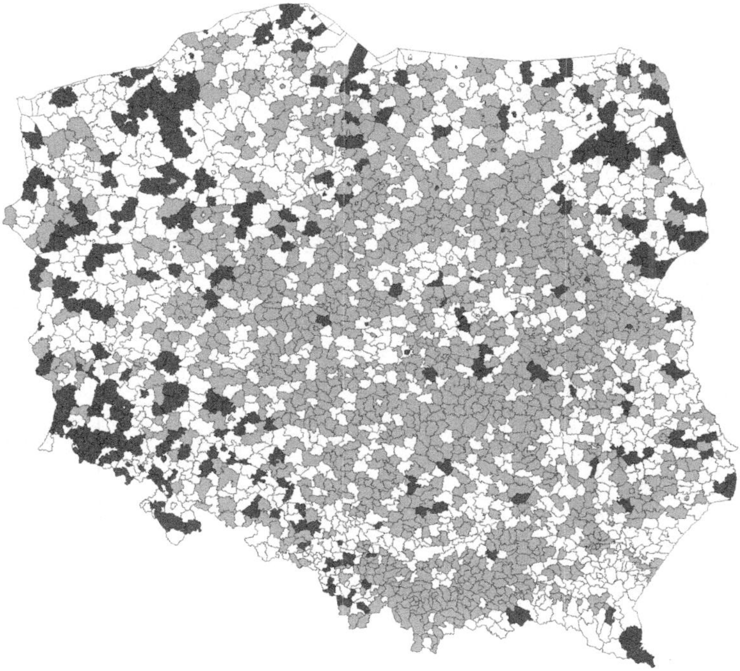

Figure 4.4 Locations of municipalities for which Spearman's rank correlation coefficient ρ values proved to be statistically significant. Positive correlations are marked light grey, while negative correlations are marked dark grey.

Source: Own study.

Figure 4.4 presents a visualisation of locations of municipalities for which the values of Spearman's rank correlation coefficient ρ proved to be statistically significant. Negative and positive correlations are marked with different colours, showing a greater concentration of negative correlations in the west of Poland and a prevalence of positive correlations in central Poland.

Considering the breakdown into voivodeships and the visualisation in the figure, considerable differences in the occurrence and correlation strength can be expected between the reduction in upper real estate tax rates in a given year and municipalities' own revenue in the subsequent year, which is reflected in Table 4.3. For two voivodeships, namely the Dolnośląskie and Zachodniopomorskie voivodeships, there are more municipalities with a negative correlation than municipalities that were positively correlated. Voivodeships with the highest percentage of municipalities for which a

Table 4.3 Results of a correlation analysis for statistically significant values of Spearman's rank correlation coefficients ρ between the reduction in upper real estate tax rates and municipalities' own revenue, broken down by voivodeships

	Negative correlations				*Positive correlations*			
Voivodeship	*Min ρ*	*Mean ρ*	*Quantity*	*Percentage (%)*	*Max*	*Mean ρ*	*Quantity*	*Percentage (%)*
Dolnośląskie	−0.89	−0.73	42	24.4	0.97	0.77	20	11.6
Kujawsko-Pomorskie	−0.78	−0.64	6	4.2	0.93	0.69	30	20.8
Lubelskie	−0.87	−0.67	6	2.7	0.97	0.71	45	20.3
Lubuskie	−0.94	−0.71	11	13.1	0.88	0.71	22	26.2
Łódzkie	−0.85	−0.77	4	2.2	0.99	0.73	96	53.3
Małopolskie	−0.73	−0.63	4	2.1	0.99	0.80	120	63.5
Mazowieckie	−0.86	−0.68	10	3.1	0.99	0.78	167	52.0
Opolskie	−0.93	−0.70	6	8.3	0.96	0.71	23	31.9
Podkarpackie	−0.79	−0.69	2	1.2	0.96	0.72	63	37.7
Podlaskie	−0.96	−0.69	12	9.8	0.96	0.74	26	21.3
Pomorskie	−0.88	−0.69	15	11.9	0.99	0.75	41	32.5
Śląskie	−0.82	−0.62	12	7.2	0.99	0.79	77	46.1
Świętokrzyskie	−0.54	−0.54	1	0.9	0.97	0.74	45	38.8
Warmińsko-Mazurskie	−0.93	−0.68	8	6.8	0.94	0.71	28	23.9
Wielkopolskie	−0.84	−0.66	7	3.0	0.99	0.76	95	40.9
Zachodniopomorskie	−0.95	−0.70	23	19.5	0.96	0.68	10	8.5

Source: Own study.

statistically significant Spearman's correlation was observed include the Małopolskie (63.5% of municipalities), Łódzkie (53.3% of municipalities), and Mazowieckie voivodeships (52.0% of municipalities).

The results of both analyses demonstrate dependencies between the reduction in upper real estate tax rates in a given year and municipalities' own revenue in the subsequent year. Statistically, the correlation proved positive and statistically significant for 908 municipalities. Analogical analyses were conducted to study the correlation between a reduction in the upper real estate tax rates and municipalities' own revenue earned from the real estate tax alone, with the results showing the existence of such a relationship. The figures to prove this fact can be found in Table 4.4.

When the municipality revenue is narrowed down to real estate tax revenue, the number of municipalities for which the correlation coefficient proved to be statistically significant grew to 1,091 (from 1,077 for municipalities' own revenue). The number of individual types of municipalities and the values of the correlation coefficients remained at a similar level even when tax revenue was removed.

To complete the analysis, it is worth including the share of natural and legal persons in a municipality's revenue. The list with a breakdown into types of municipalities is provided in Table 4.5. For each type of municipality, the percentage of municipalities with a statistically significant negative correlation was, on average, 1.78 times lower (from 1.15 to 2.66 times lower) for natural persons than for legal persons. At the same time, the percentage of municipalities with a statistically significant positive correlation was 3%–18% higher for natural persons (compared to legal persons). For nearly 58% of urban municipalities, after narrowing down to natural persons, the correlation dependence proved to be significant and positive, which is also true for almost half (47%, to be precise) of the cities with county rights.

Figure 4.5 presents a visualisation of locations of municipalities for which the values of Spearman's rank correlation coefficient ρ, narrowed down to natural and legal persons, respectively, proved to be statistically significant. When it comes to reductions in upper tax rates and own revenue earned from natural persons, municipalities with identified positive correlations merge into clusters that, on the one hand, may prove that the location is attractive (not only in terms of tax) and, on the other hand, may confirm the existence of tax competition (see Section 4.3). Municipalities with a positive Spearman's correlation coefficient determined based on data from legal persons are more dispersed. There are many more such municipalities near Poland's eastern border, which may prove the existence of preferential conditions for companies located there.

The results shown in this section demonstrate the existence of dependencies between the reduction in upper real estate tax rates and a municipality's selected or total revenue in the subsequent year. Correlations are not

Table 4.4 Descriptive statistics for statistically significant values of Spearman's rank correlation coefficients ρ between the reduction in the upper real estate tax rates and municipalities' own revenue from the real estate tax, broken down by the type of municipality

		Number	*Percentage*	*Minimum*	*First quartile*	*Median*	*Mean*	*Third quartile*	*Maximum*
Negative values ρ	POLAND	192	7.50%	−0.99	−0.78	−0.69	−0.70	−0.61	−0.54
	RM	95	6.00%	−0.99	−0.78	−0.69	−0.70	−0.60	−0.54
	URM	50	7.70%	−0.93	−0.79	−0.67	−0.70	−0.60	−0.54
	UM	35	14.50%	−0.94	−0.81	−0.71	−0.73	−0.64	−0.54
	CCR	12	18.20%	−0.85	−0.74	−0.68	−0.68	−0.62	−0.56
Positive values ρ	POLAND	899	35.30%	0.54	0.65	0.76	0.76	0.86	1.00
	RM	588	37.00%	0.54	0.65	0.76	0.76	0.86	1.00
	URM	201	30.80%	0.54	0.63	0.72	0.74	0.85	0.99
	UM	89	36.80%	0.54	0.70	0.80	0.79	0.88	0.98
	CCR	21	31.80%	0.56	0.72	0.83	0.81	0.92	0.99

Source: Own study.

Table 4.5 Descriptive statistics for statistically significant values of Spearman's rank correlation coefficients ρ between the reduction in the upper real estate tax rates and municipalities' own revenue from the real estate tax, broken down by the type of municipality and the share of natural and legal persons (in %)

		POLAND	*RM*	*URM*	*UM*	*CCR*
Negative values ρ	Total	6.60	4.90	7.80	12.00	16.70
	Natural persons	6.00	4.00	8.50	14.90	10.90
	Legal persons	11.30	10.60	9.70	20.80	20.00
Positive values ρ	Total	35.60	37.80	31.10	34.30	33.30
	Natural persons	40.30	39.20	37.60	57.80	47.30
	Legal persons	34.60	36.00	29.50	39.60	34.50

Source: Own study.

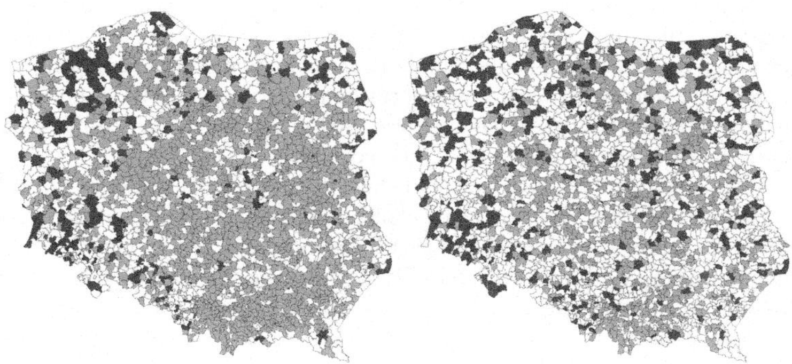

Figure 4.5 Locations of municipalities for which the values of Spearman's rank correlation coefficient ρ narrowed down to natural persons (on the left) and legal persons (on the right) proved to be statistically significant. Positive correlations are marked light grey, while negative correlations are marked dark grey.

Source: Own study.

constant throughout Poland and differ considerably among voivodeships. External factors, such as tax competition, also mitigate the strength of the effect. Reductions in upper real estate tax rates affect the behaviour of natural persons more than legal persons. Optimising the size of reductions to maximise municipality revenue remains an open issue.

4.3 Municipal tax competition and the consequences thereof

In the context of local government units, tax competition is understood as the adaptation of the tax policy of a local government unit to fiscal actions undertaken by neighbouring units or, more generally, competitive units (Łukomska and Swianiewicz, 2015). Tax policy usually reduces tax rates to attract investors or new residents. Increasing the number of natural or legal persons operating in a given municipality not only affects the increase in real estate tax revenue (investments in the market of residential and commercial real estate, changes in land classification, and new building structures related to the business activity) but also indirectly affects earnings from the income tax (actions by the municipality may encourage residents and business owners to reside and carry on business activities in the municipality; the amount of their income affects the municipality's earnings from the municipality's share in PIT and CIT taxes). On a nationwide level, it is hard to identify competitive municipalities since even local government units that are very distant from each other may compete in taxes. For example, large Polish cities, such as Kraków and Warsaw, are often depicted as competing when it comes to academic attractiveness, which is vital in winning the interest of students and prospective students, while the simplest approximation of fiscal competitiveness in the context of local government units is to consider the immediate neighbourhood. This understanding was used to analyse the tax competition issue, as described in the results in this section.

One method of verifying the tax competition of municipalities in Poland was a questionnaire survey targeted at municipalities. Question 9 of the questionnaire survey concerned the impact of the rates charged by neighbouring municipalities on tax rate decisions. The respondents answered either as legal persons or as natural persons, broken down by the type of municipality. Collated answers are presented in Figures 4.6 and 4.7. Opinions of municipalities

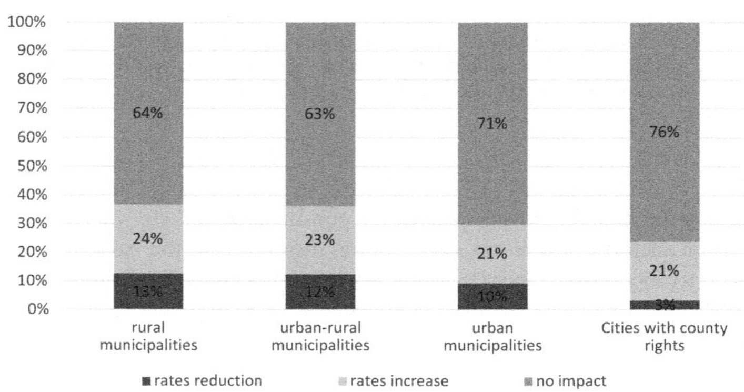

Figure 4.6 The percentage of positive responses to the question of how tax rates in neighbouring municipalities affect the rates in a given municipality (broken down by municipality type).

Source: Own study based on a survey sent to the municipalities.

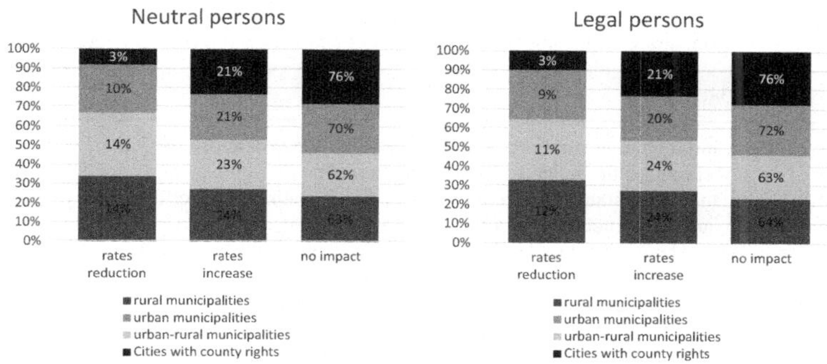

Figure 4.7 The percentage of municipalities claiming that tax rates in neighbouring municipalities do not affect the rates fixed in a given municipality (broken down by natural and legal persons and by municipality type).

Source: Own study based on a survey sent to the municipalities.

on the impact of the rate in neighbouring municipalities on the rate increase or decrease were taken into account, along with the assertion that tax rates in neighbouring municipalities do not affect rates in a given municipality.

Responses from representatives of the municipalities to the questions asked in the questionnaire survey suggest a lack of tax competition among Polish municipalities. The vast majority of municipalities (62%–76%) argue that the rates of neighbouring municipalities do not affect their decisions related to tax rates (both for natural and legal persons). Therefore, the tax competition phenomenon hypothesis among Polish municipalities was not proven or refuted based on the respondents' opinions. Such opinions were confronted with complex data from SP-1 real estate tax returns for 2020, drawn up by the tax authorities competent for that tax. Selected sections listed in Table 4.6 were analysed.

The analysis compared tax rates charged in a given municipality with the average tax rate in directly neighbouring municipalities. Given that many municipalities charge maximum rates, the distribution of rates heavily skews to the left. Figure 4.8 shows box plots demonstrating the rates charged by the municipalities for selected sections. The visualisation is narrowed down to the sections that support the tax competition phenomenon the most and simultaneously account for the highest percentage of municipality revenue. These are:

- Section 1.1 – land related to running a business activity, regardless of how it is classified in the land and building register (the lowest rate is 0.35 PLN/sq.m., the highest rate is 0.95 PLN/sq.m., with a median of 0.88 PLN/sq.m.);

Table 4.6 Sections of the real estate tax considered during the analysis of tax competition, along with statistically significant Spearman's correlation coefficients ρ

Symbol	*Description*	*ρ*
1.1	Land related to running a business activity, regardless of how it is classified in the land and building register	0.54
1.2	Land under standing surface water or flowing surface water of lakes and constructed reservoirs	0.22
1.3	Other land including land used for paid statutory public benefit activities by public benefit organisations	0.60
1.4	Undeveloped land within the regeneration area referred to in the Act of 9 October 2015 on Regeneration (Journal of Laws of 2017, item 1023, as amended) and located in areas for which the local development plan stipulates that the land will be designated for residential, commercial, or mixed-use development, comprising only such types of development if a period of four years has passed since the effective date of this plan concerning such land, and the construction has not been completed during this time by the provisions of the construction law	0.26
1.5	Residential buildings	0.59
1.6	Buildings related to the conduct of business activities and residential buildings or parts thereof used for the conduct of business activities	0.66
1.7	Buildings occupied for the conduct of business activities in the field of trade in certified seeds	0.30
1.8	Buildings related to the provision of health services within the meaning of the provisions on medical activities, occupied by entities which provide such services	0.24
1.9	Other buildings including land used for paid statutory public benefit activities by public benefit organisations	0.54
1.10	Structures	

Source: Own study based on the SP-1 Tax Return part 2.

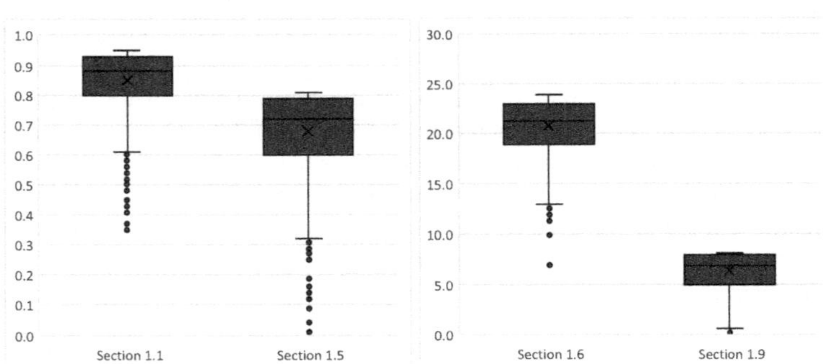

Figure 4.8 Distribution of tax rates adopted by municipalities in 2020 in four selected sections.

Source: Own study.

- Section 1.5 – residential buildings (the lowest rate is 0.01 PLN/sq.m., the highest rate is 0.81 PLN/sq.m., with a median of 0.72 PLN/sq.m.);
- Section 1.6 – buildings related to conducting business activities and residential buildings or parts thereof used for conducting business activities (the lowest rate is 6.86 PLN/sq.m., the highest rate is 23.90 PLN/sq.m., with a median of 21.20 PLN/sq.m.);
- Section 1.9 – other buildings, including land used for paid statutory public benefit activities by public benefit organisations (the lowest rate is 0.15 PLN/sq.m., the highest rate is 8.05 PLN/sq.m., with a median of 6.87 PLN/sq.m.).

The Spearman's correlation was used to compare the rates adopted by municipalities with the mean tax rate in directly neighbouring municipalities, an approach which, considering the specific nature of rate distribution, is more suitable than Pearson's linear correlation. The existence of correlation dependencies was verified at the significance level of 0.05, and the hypothesis of the tax competition phenomenon was proven for all the sections other than the tax rate on structures (Section 1.10), with only one municipality not approving the upper rate of the tax on structures. Thus, it is difficult to speak about tax competition in this case.

The strongest correlation can be observed for sections comprising real estate tax on buildings related to business activity ($\rho = 0.66$). A relatively strong dependence can also be found for the real estate tax on residential buildings ($\rho = 0.59$) and other buildings ($\rho = 0.54$), as well as tax on land related to the conduct of business activity ($\rho = 0.54$). The distribution of tax rates approved by municipalities in 2020 for the four mentioned sections was shown on maps in Figures 4.9-4.12. The municipality clusters with similar colours prove standard behaviour models when it comes to fixing the tax rates.

The maps in Figures 4.9–4.12 show a significant disproportion between tax rates approved by individual municipalities, which can implicate differences in the tax competition phenomenon in various parts of the country.

Table 4.7 presents vital information about the tax rates and the tax competition phenomenon broken down by voivodeships, with only the four sections addressed in this section. The highest approved tax rates in each voivodeship were equal (*max*. column), but the lowest and mean rates (*min* and *mean* columns) differed considerably. In each of the four sections, the highest mean tax rate is recorded for the Dolnośląskie voivodeship, while the Mazowieckie voivodeship received the highest Spearman's correlation coefficient ρ. The tax competition phenomenon was not proven for all the voivodeships: for the Lubuskie, Opolskie, and Świętokrzyskie voivodeships, in two out of four cases, Spearman's correlation coefficient ρ proved to be statistically insignificant (at the significance level of 0.05).

Based on the results of analyses, the cause of such strong convergence in the fixing of tax rates cannot be determined. The results are sufficient to conclude

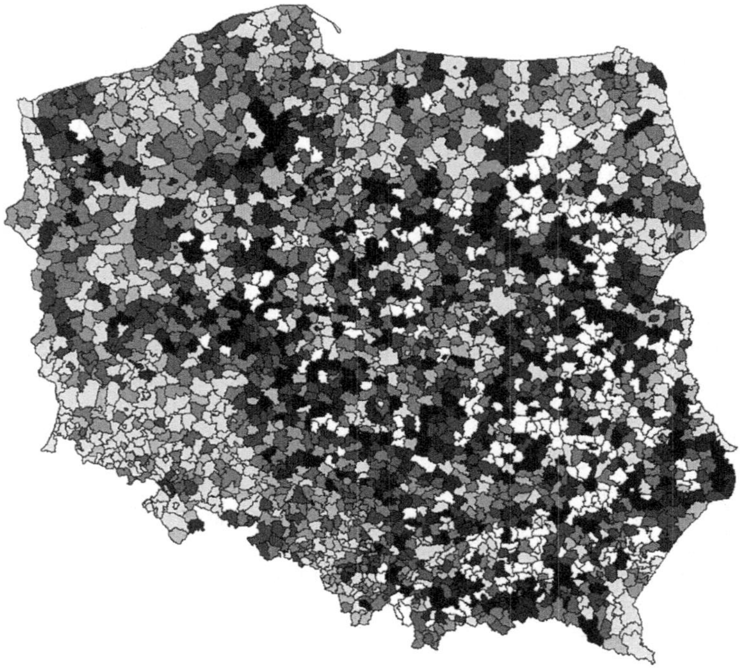

Figure 4.9 The amount of tax rates on land related to conducting business activities as adopted by municipalities in 2020. Greyscale from the lowest flat rate of 0.35 PLN/sq.m. (white) to the highest flat rate of 0.95 PLN/sq.m. (black).

Source: Own study.

that the phenomenon of joint determination of rates does occur, namely that there is a co-dependence between the fixed rates and the mean rates in neighbouring municipalities. Perhaps there are common reasons for the reduction in the upper tax rates that so many municipalities have applied. However, considering the number of municipalities (2,477 municipalities in 2020), this is highly unlikely. One of the possible and most apparent explanations is the tax competition phenomenon. The analysis results do not attest to the tax competition phenomenon – it is a phenomenon that should be studied over a more extended period and not just based on one year's data. Still, the statistical significance of Spearman's correlation coefficients provides strong arguments to claim that municipalities, consciously or not, take note of the tax rates in neighbouring municipalities and, in many cases, adjust their tax policy to match the policies of their neighbours.

As mentioned in this section and in Chapter 1 of the monograph, municipalities compete in terms of tax rates to establish an area that would be attractive to potential investors or residents, encouraging them to move or expand

Figure 4.10 The amount of tax rates on residential buildings as adopted by municipalities in 2020. Greyscale from the lowest flat rate of 0.01 PLN/sq.m. (white) to the highest flat rate of 0.81 PLN/sq.m. (black).

Source: Own study.

their business to a specific location. Such actions are usually motivated by the willingness to increase the tax base and other social and economic purposes, such as stimulating the establishment of new workplaces.

Real estate tax seems to be potentially less susceptible to tax competition (compared to, e.g. tax on means of transport), primarily due to the lack of mobility of the objects of taxation and limitations in shaping the tax rates. However, in the continued study, based on the existing results, it should be stated that such competition does exist, even if only to a certain extent.

During the focus study, representatives of the local government (executive branch) argue that being located on the outskirts of a larger city is a significant factor contributing to the potential existence of tax competition. In such a situation, residents may live in a smaller municipality and pay lower real estate taxes while enjoying extensive city infrastructure. The executive branch believes that the willingness to increase the tax base frequently motivates competition among municipalities regarding tax rates. However, they mention that it is not so much

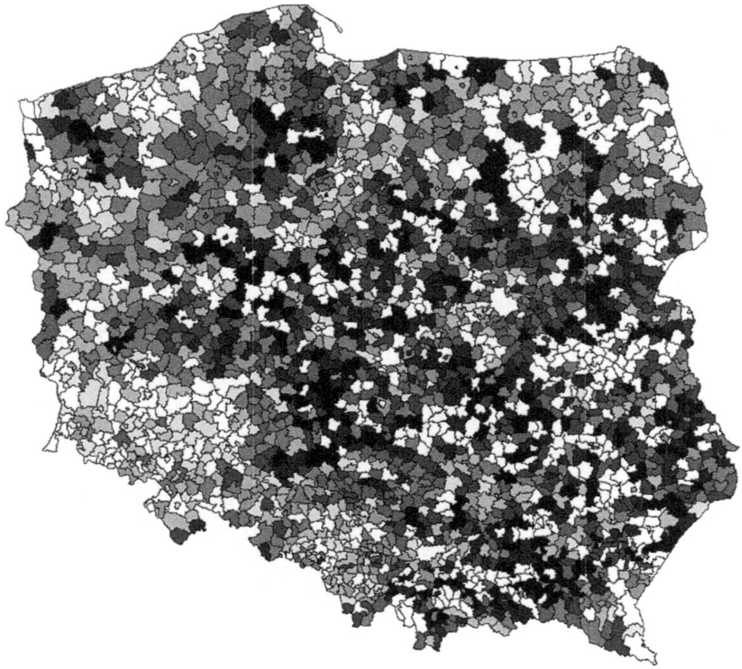

Figure 4.11 The amount of tax rates on buildings related to conducting business activities as adopted by municipalities in 2020. Greyscale from the lowest flat rate of 6.86 PLN/sq.m. (white) to the highest flat rate of 23.90 PLN/sq.m. (black).

Source: Own study.

the tax rates but the standards of living or standards of public services offered by a given local government unit that encourages residents to select a specific location, stressing that real estate tax is a crucial local tax, and when it comes to smaller, less affluent municipalities, a reduction in tax rates would have a significant negative impact on the revenue of local government units.

Most respondents do not notice the existence of more extensive tax competition, at least not when it comes to tax rates alone. From the taxpayers' perspective, what attracts businesses is the exemption from taxes for a certain period – although they argue that measures aimed at establishing technical and social infrastructure are much more critical. The respondents view the tax rate reduction in the context of public relations as intended to build the image of a municipality that charges lower taxes. Table 4.8 presents aspects related to tax competition mentioned by the executive branch, statements of authorities of the municipalities, and expected consequences of the phenomena mentioned.

Figure 4.12 The amount of tax rates on other buildings as adopted by municipalities in 2020. Greyscale from the lowest flat rate of 0.15 PLN/sq.m. (white) to the highest flat rate of 8.05 PLN/sq.m. (black).

Source: Own study.

As mentioned at the beginning of the section, the issue of tax competition was also addressed in questionnaire surveys conducted among municipalities and residents. From the perspective of residents, tax competition does not seem to be a significant factor affecting the choice of place to live, and on average, 60% of residents declared that they would not be willing to change their place of residence to reduce tax charges. Such responses differ slightly depending on the type of municipality (55% for urban municipalities and 62%–65% for other types of municipalities).

At the same time, 55% of surveyed residents would be willing to change their place of establishment of their business to pay lower taxes. The willingness to change the place of establishment is thus slightly lower among the persons who conduct business activity, but such people also pay higher tax charges. Considering the tax rates for enterprises, compared to those charged from natural persons, it still seems that this percentage of declarations is not very extensive.

Table 4.7 Descriptive statistics on the rates for selected tax sections determined in individual voivodeships with statistically significant Spearman's correlation coefficients ρ related to the tax competition

Voivodeship	*Land related to running a business activity (Section 1.1)*				*Residential buildings (Section 1.5)*			
	Min	*Mean*	*Max*	*ρ*	*Min*	*Mean*	*Max*	*ρ*
Dolnośląskie	0.80	0.93	0.95	0.19	0.57	0.79	0.81	0.26
Kujawsko-Pomorskie	0.55	0.85	0.95	×	0.16	0.67	0.81	0.42
Lubelskie	0.37	0.80	0.95	0.34	0.02	0.61	0.81	0.18
Lubuskie	0.74	0.90	0.95	0.29	0.42	0.76	0.81	×
Łódzkie	0.54	0.83	0.95	0.38	0.10	0.60	0.81	0.22
Małopolskie	0.41	0.81	0.95	0.47	0.05	0.63	0.81	0.48
Mazowieckie	0.44	0.81	0.95	0.53	0.01	0.61	0.81	0.54
Opolskie	0.70	0.89	0.95	0.30	0.55	0.76	0.81	×
Podkarpackie	0.42	0.81	0.95	0.39	0.10	0.60	0.81	0.53
Podlaskie	0.35	0.85	0.95	0.44	0.01	0.70	0.81	0.42
Pomorskie	0.74	0.90	0.95	0.22	0.50	0.75	0.81	0.43
Śląskie	0.68	0.89	0.95	0.43	0.31	0.74	0.81	0.37
Świętokrzyskie	0.56	0.83	0.95	0.42	0.04	0.59	0.81	×
Warmińsko-Mazurskie	0.61	0.89	0.95	0.19	0.49	0.75	0.81	×
Wielkopolskie	0.64	0.85	0.95	0.39	0.29	0.70	0.81	0.59
Zachodniopomorskie	0.52	0.90	0.95	0.44	0.49	0.75	0.81	0.40

Voivodeship	*Buildings related to running a business activity (Section 1.6)*				*Other buildings (Section 1.9)*			
	Min	*Mean*	*Max*	*ρ*	*Min*	*Mean*	*Max*	*ρ*
Dolnośląskie	19.20	23.24	23.90	0.25	1.60	7.46	8.05	0.25
Kujawsko-Pomorskie	14.85	21.05	23.90	0.45	0.60	6.78	8.05	0.28
Lubelskie	12.50	19.37	23.90	0.51	0.35	5.81	8.05	0.39
Lubuskie	16.00	22.23	23.90	0.34	1.40	6.90	8.05	×
Łódzkie	14.40	19.93	23.90	0.49	1.83	6.19	8.05	0.32
Małopolskie	6.86	19.44	23.90	0.58	1.10	5.84	8.05	0.30
Mazowieckie	11.90	19.73	23.90	0.65	1.00	5.76	8.05	0.54
Opolskie	17.00	21.86	23.90	0.33	4.00	6.34	8.05	×
Podkarpackie	9.90	19.47	23.90	0.46	0.15	5.02	8.05	0.54
Podlaskie	10.00	20.91	23.90	0.46	2.81	6.76	8.05	0.49
Pomorskie	17.00	21.99	23.90	0.55	2.50	7.30	8.05	0.23
Śląskie	16.79	22.18	23.90	0.59	3.80	6.99	8.05	0.41
Świętokrzyskie	13.05	20.05	23.90	0.59	0.94	5.45	8.05	×
Warmińsko-Mazurskie	16.20	21.71	23.90	0.26	2.33	7.28	8.05	0.21
Wielkopolskie	14.30	20.63	23.90	0.57	2.79	6.30	8.05	0.55
Zachodniopomorskie	15.22	22.35	23.90	0.46	2.80	7.18	8.05	0.34

Source: Own study.

Municipalities also do not see tax rates as an effective tool for encouraging residents to settle in a given area. Around 40% of municipalities view such a contribution as average, regardless of whether they are rural, urban-rural, or cities with county rights.

The questionnaire survey demonstrates that municipalities see the potential to encourage businesses with tax rates. This is particularly true of cities with county rights, with 50% of such cities responding that tax preferences have a high or very high potential to attract the establishment of new businesses in that location (Figure 4.13). This potential is not that considerable when it comes to existing businesses.

What comes across as exciting and valuable in the context of the previous section is that most correspondents from the surveyed municipalities perceive tax preferences more as a tool that builds the tax base and ensures higher tax revenue in the future. Regarding the type of municipality, 77% to 84% of municipalities answered that tax preferences affect future budget revenue to an average, high, or very high extent (Figure 4.14). In particular, this is true of urban municipalities and urban-rural municipalities.

Table 4.8 Results of the focus study of local tax competition

Local tax competition		
Aspect addressed	*Statement of the executive*	*Expected consequences*
There is a slight differentiation of real estate tax rates among municipalities.	"In a household's budget, the annual tax is around PLN 200-300. So if we pay PLN 300 for the building alone and the next municipality charges PLN 330 a year then [...] then no one is interested about the tax being slightly higher or lower".	Lack of impact of real estate tax rates on decisions made by residents concerning settlement in a given municipality
Location as a critical factor determining tax competition	"This [phenomenon] is typical. I represent a medium-sized town and see that some municipalities, especially suburban municipalities, try to compete with us in terms of the amount of real estate tax. [...] municipalities do not lower [real estate tax]. When they increase the tax, they keep it within certain limits to remain competitive". "As for municipalities with potential [municipalities around big cities], such municipalities can compete with urban areas because of the close vicinity, jobs and the potential to grow".	Smaller municipalities wishing to compete with big cities might charge lower rates than bigger cities (especially on the outskirts of a big city)
Willingness to increase the tax base	"[...] Municipalities are interested in having as many potential residents as possible because everybody knows that real estate tax is the source of budget revenue of each local government authority."	Offering incentives to settle in areas that have not provided urban infrastructure to date
Real estate tax as a source of municipality revenue	"[...] we happen to have [...] tiny rural municipalities with pre-determined real estate tax at the highest rates, and larger cities [...] either differentiate the tax or not always charge it at the highest rates".	With less affluent municipalities, a rate reduction could result in an excessive decrease in revenue.

(*Continued*)

Table 4.8 (Continued)

Local tax competition		
Aspect addressed	*Statement of the executive*	*Expected consequences*
Ability to earn revenue from other sources	"[…] for small municipalities […] real estate tax is the main and fundamental element of municipality revenue. […]. Big cities […] with economic zones or other possibilities of earning revenue can diversify revenue and reduce the rates or not charge maximum rates". "[…] if an industrial zone is to be developed, there are opportunities. […] you need a buffer in your budget to reduce the taxes for one or two years". "I wasn't even tempted to compare tax rates […] we know that we can't bite off more than we can chew, and if the budget doesn't hold well, then the tax rates cannot be lower".	Municipalities that can find funds from other sources may consider a rate reduction; in other cases, the issue of tax competition fades into the background.
Tax reliefs	"There is not […] much competition. […] taxes are increased because we need revenue, but we also offer reliefs as incentives or tax exemptions for 3–5 years or a year, depending on the type of business". "We offer tax reliefs. As for new businesses that want to become established in our economic zone, we have real estate tax exemptions for those who buy land from us".	An increase in tax reliefs may encourage businesses to become established in a given municipality.
The level of public services and infrastructure as an incentive to settle in a given municipality	"If you pay, for example, PLN 10,000 in real estate tax and run an enterprise hiring several or dozens of employees […], and the next municipality charges PLN 11,000 in tax per year, this PLN 1,000 in savings […] will not be enough to make you move. What makes businesses move […] are completely different elements, such as access to an expressway, […] an established economic zone with all utilities […] low resident resistance [to investments] or high unemployment in the area […] Residents look for forests, peace, or a nursery school nearby".	The need to increase the quality of public services and investments in infrastructure does not lead to a reduction in rates.

Source: own study.

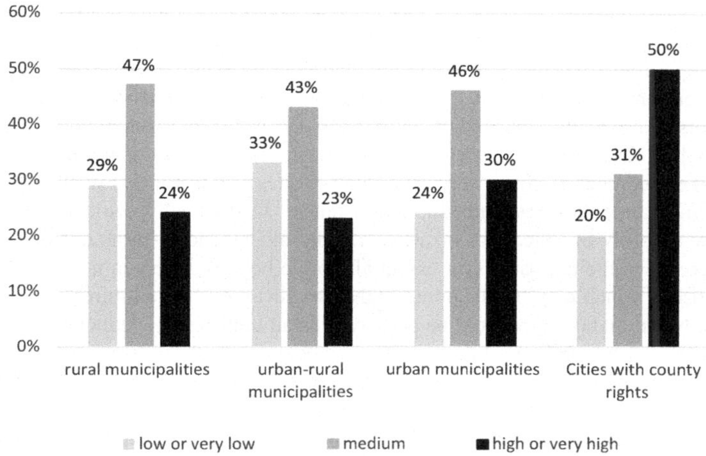

Figure 4.13 An assessment of the impact of the preferential taxation with real estate tax as a location incentive for businesses.

Source: Own study based on survey data (municipalities).

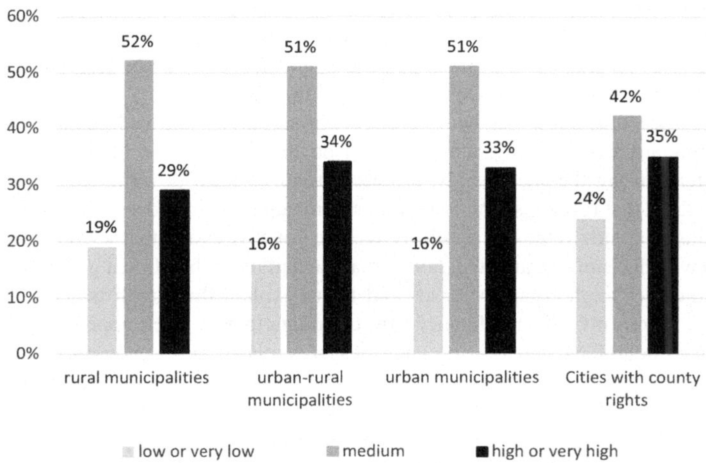

Figure 4.14 An assessment of the impact of the preferential taxation with real estate tax as a source of increasing budget revenue from real estate tax in the future.

Source: Own study based on survey data (municipalities).

Questionnaire surveys and focus studies are not enough to give an unambiguous answer to the research questions about the existence of tax competition regarding real estate tax, and they have not produced any resolutions in this regard. On the one hand, local governments do not see tax charges, especially imposed on natural persons, as essential enough to pursue a policy based on tax competition. In contrast, residents, both natural persons and entrepreneurs, do not see real estate tax rates as a factor that would make them change their residence or establishment. Undoubtedly, we deal with a low mobility of objects of taxation. On the other hand, it turns out that an increase in the tax base is an essential motive behind the potential tax competition, which may translate into higher tax revenues in the future. Competing based on tax rates could be perceived as an unnecessary reduction in tax revenue, while offering high-quality technical or social infrastructure could be an alternative solution as part of the competition in this regard, yet this requires certain funds. A dilemma, essential from the perspective of the financial management of municipalities, presents itself here: what should the priority be – the current horizon or perhaps the medium- or long-term horizon?

4.4 The concept of an average voter

According to the concept of an average voter, the authority's goal is not to implement essential ideas but to win voters. Hence, the authority adjusts its policy to the views of voters. Residents vote for candidates whose views are the most acceptable to them. When the candidates take office, they calculate potential voters' wins and losses when making decisions.

When this study was being drafted, we assumed that local governments formulate electoral programmes based on the expectations of the average voter. During the focus study, representatives of local governments clearly declared that residents' opinions were significant to them and that they tried to adjust tax rates to the budget of the average voter, stressing that voters always viewed decisions related to a tax increase as unfavourable. Local government authorities explain tax increases and try to explain them with benefits that result from investments financed by the municipality. Such approaches are often undertaken as part of broader measures related to the economic education of residents. Table 4.9 presents aspects related to the average voter model mentioned by the executive branch, statements of authorities of municipalities, and the expected consequences of the aspects addressed.

According to the questionnaire surveys, most municipalities view the tax charges imposed on residents as average. This mainly applies to rural, urban, and urban-rural municipalities. Cities with county rights stand out here, with 31% of the municipalities claiming the tax imposed was high (Figure 4.15).

Preferences or reductions in tax rates did not significantly improve residents' economic situation (Figure 4.16), at least from the perspective of municipalities. This is because the real estate tax is not the source of considerable household tax charges.

Table 4.9 Results of the focus study of the average voter model

	Average voter model	
Aspect addressed	*Statement of the executive*	*Expected consequences*
Residents' opinions are essential to the authorities, even more important than those of the legislative body.	"[…] we also have to account for the aspirations and expectations of our residents and the mean level of earnings. The real estate tax is a levy, and each of our residents has to pay that levy one way or the other". "I care more about residents' opinions than councillors' opinions". "I pay much attention to residents' opinions and our consequent follow-up actions".	The executive body will take residents' opinions when determining the rates.
The need to adjust tax rates to the financial capacity of the average voter	"[…] we confront the [tax increase] with general information about the affluence of our residents, […] because adoption of maximum rates in a situation when our residents are unable to pay them will result in budget deficits in the form of unpaid real estate tax".	The rates proposed by the executive body in the draft resolution shall depend on the affluence of municipality residents.
Negative perception of each tax increase by residents	"I realise that such decisions [tax increases] are difficult". "Increasing taxes is always an unpopular decision".	The tax rates will be increased only when necessary (if a deficit in the municipality budget has to be covered).
The need for economic education of residents	"We translate the tasks and investments into a language of benefits for our residents, which, to an extent, compensates for the tax increases. There is always a group of disgruntled residents". "We make such decisions by trying to respond to the residents' views, but we also want to shape such views to a certain extent". "We listen to what residents say, but we probably all have the same experience: residents expect many investments but would not like to pay tax at all, so we promote education. […] we try to explain to the residents […] what they actually get from the tax". "[…] we are definitely missing education on local government finances in Poland, […] and residents think that we have money stashed away in bags and do not want to do anything, so by showing them how many investments are being implemented, we are saying that the investments are also carried out thanks to the real estate tax". "We try to educate residents this way, […] we also run educational campaigns at schools, […] we show what the budget is composed of, why the tax is important and why we share".	Each increase will require educational activity and making residents aware of the benefits that the increase will translate to in public services and investments.

Source: Own study.

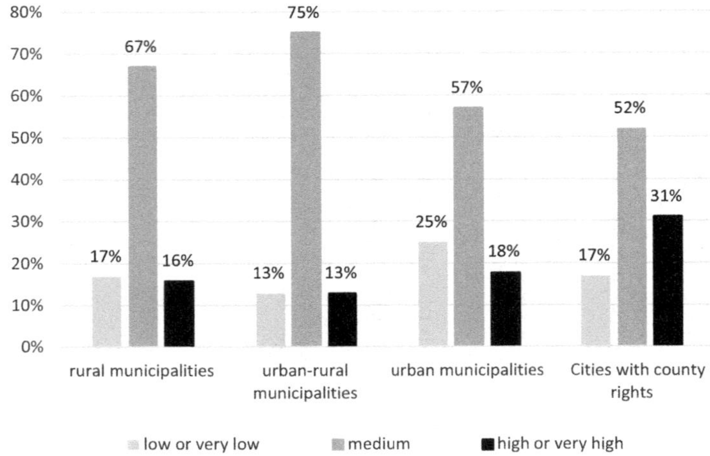

Figure 4.15 Are the real estate taxes imposed on the public in your municipality low, medium, or high, in your opinion?

Source: Own study based on survey data (municipalities).

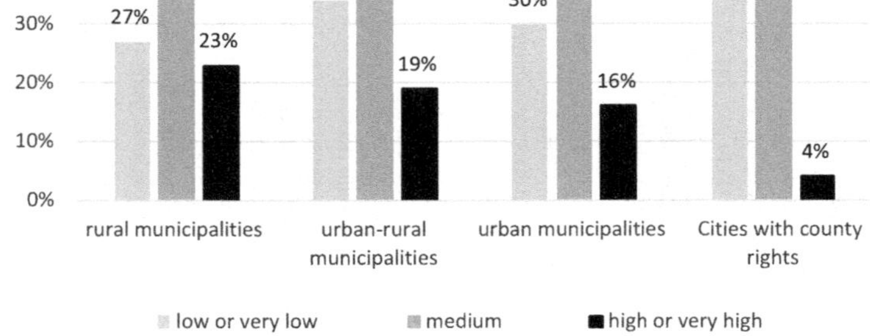

Figure 4.16 Assessment of the impact of preferential taxation with real estate tax as a tool to improve the economic situation of residents.

Source: Own study based on survey data (municipalities).

Given the above, municipalities do not view the real estate tax rates as high or as particularly affecting the situation of residents (natural persons). Although, as the results of the focus studies show, residents unwillingly accept tax increases, it is hard to expect local governments to consider residents' preferences in this scope. This mainly results from the distribution of burdens over many taxpayers. Although real estate tax is the leading tax imposed by local governments, it is not a tool of an intensive tax policy.

D. Black's theory that local politicians fulfil the needs of median voters (1948; Piwowarski, 2014; Łukomska and Swianiewicz, 2015) cannot, therefore, be empirically proven. This mainly results from the relatively low real estate tax charges.

4.5 Political (electoral) cycle

The imminent elections can impact decisions made by local government authorities, at the very least producing stimuli to postpone unpopular decisions until after the elections. A significant increase in tax rates could be viewed as an unpopular decision. This prompted the formulation of the following study question: Does the political cycle affect decisions made on real estate tax rates?

The respondents generally agreed that the willingness to raise taxes decreased in the pre-election period. At the same time, some of them believed that the level of rates was not that important during the election campaign. They also stressed that opposition councillors have not welcomed each proposal to increase rates. Table 4.10 presents aspects related to the political

Table 4.10 Results of the focus study on the political business cycle

Political business cycle		
Aspect addressed	*Statement of the executive*	*Expected consequences*
Low tax rates are related to the image of the municipality and the authorities.	"This is a PR trick; [...] a small section of that tax palette is actually cheaper, [...] this phenomenon is hardly noticeable, but it is present".	The imminence of the local government elections can be a stimulus to reduce, or at least not to raise, tax rates.
The need to approve tax rates by Municipal Councils by way of a resolution	"We always make comparisons with neighbouring cities, [to have] arguments [...] for the councillors, because in the end, it is they who have to approve the taxes. [...] the [political] burden is [...] transferred to the mayor, [...] which is a challenge in the last year of their term in office".	The level of the tax rates could be an element of the competition between the executive and legislative branches, but it also favours populism.

(*Continued*)

Table 4.10 (Continued)

Political business cycle		
Aspect addressed	*Statement of the executive*	*Expected consequences*
Relations between the executive and legislative branch	"[…] I had a minority in the Council for the entire term of office, and unfortunately, I could not push forward several projects because they were […] blocked at any price, just for the sake of being blocked".	The lack of trust in the executive and legislative branches favours decision-making that is attractive to the voters
A lower tendency to raise tax rates in the pre-election period	"[…] the term of office cycle impacts the scale or willingness to make tax decisions. Obviously, the closer the elections, the more self-restraint there is in making bolder tax decisions […]. […] Everyone is rather afraid of a populist witch-hunt". "The closer the elections, the more difficult it is to make such tax decisions [increase the rates]". "[…] the [political premises] are hugely important, so we have to deal with every political situation".	Authorities avoid unpopular decisions.
Tax rates are an element used in the election campaign by the opposition	"I […] would raise [the tax rates] each year if that burden rested on me and myself alone, […] looking at politics, […] no one thinks about taxes during elections. The campaign period is unique". "As for our decisions […] they largely affect the relations between the Mayor and the Council, because if you work with a Council that is fully in opposition […] regardless of the consequences for the city and its development, then […] political, more populist decisions are made. […] In such cases, even the best ideas and the most reasonable tax increases will not be approved because each decision by the mayor must be negated. If […] you co-operate with the Council and have […] your councillors, […] but the other councillors are also open and able to understand your arguments, then it starts to make sense".	Authorities avoid unpopular decisions.

Source: Own study.

business cycle mentioned by the executive branch, statements of authorities of the municipalities, and the expected consequences of the aspects addressed.

The concept of the political business cycle is connected, to a certain extent, with the concept of the average voter in the sense that the imminence of elections increases the tendency to move political programmes closer towards the median voter. As mentioned earlier, neither voters nor the municipalities perceive real estate tax rates as a factor providing particular incentives related to the place of residence or establishment or even a factor affecting taxpayers' economic and financial situation. However, the promise of a rate reduction can influence voters' decisions at the ballot box. On average, around 60% of the respondents said that declared changes in tax rates affect their electoral choices, with the highest percentage of such persons living in rural municipalities.

What is essential is that the impact of the direction of changes is not unambiguous. However, 45%–55% of residents felt that the lower the taxes, the better, and 11%–15% of the residents replied that the higher the taxes, the better (Figure 4.17). For 11%–20% of residents, the real estate tax rate level was irrelevant when making electoral decisions.

Regarding the theories of the political business cycle presented in Chapter 1, it should be primarily concluded that they mainly pertain to unemployment and inflation, making it hard to directly translate them into decisions on real estate tax rates in the municipalities. Indeed, increasing tax rates is an unpopular decision that does not bring new voters, especially since voters expect taxes to go down, even if such charges hardly affect their household budget.

K. Rogoff argued that the authorities may achieve their political goals by increasing transfers (1990). A decision to decrease (or not increase) taxes in the pre-election period could be viewed as the equivalent of such a transfer and a sign of a political cycle, especially since the focus study clearly proves the unwillingness to raise taxes in the pre-election period. This is in line with the results of research by A. Alesina and M. Paradisi (2017), M.L. da Fonseca (2020), and M. Klien (2015).

A. Alesina, N. Roubini, and G.D. Cohen, in turn, assumed that voters are guided by their individual preferences, which translates to support for the party that is more useful for voters (1997). In this approach, both an increase and decrease in taxes could be perceived favourably (cf. Figure 4.17).

4.6 Partisan political model

The partisan political model assumes that local tax policy is primarily determined by politicians' ideology, which results from their membership in a specific political party. As part of the research, an assumption was made that political preferences at the local government level could be less important than at the central level, especially concerning the executive branch.

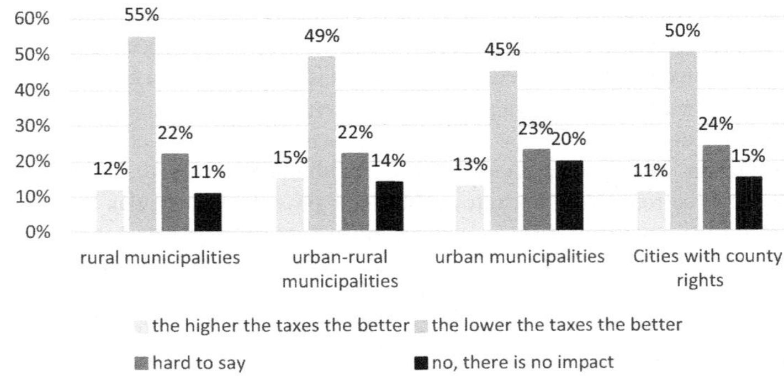

Figure 4.17 Does municipal candidates' stated decrease/increase in real estate tax impact your decision to vote for them?

Source: Own study based on survey data (residents).

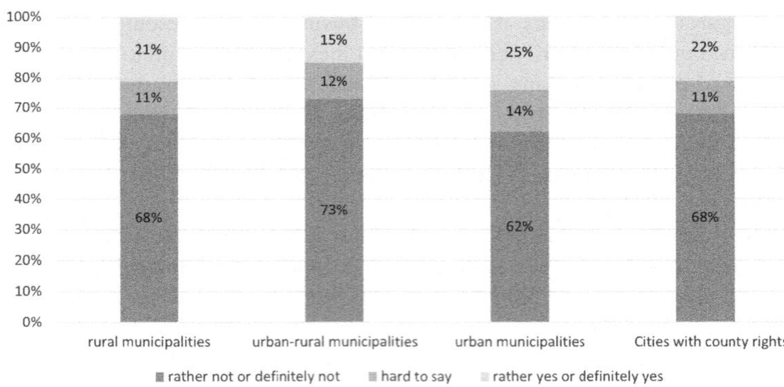

Figure 4.18 Were draft resolutions on real estate tax on land in their particular stages (initial draft, meeting of a competent commission, municipal council session) adopted in your municipality after a turbulent discussion?

Source: Own study based on survey data (municipalities).

Most respondents believe that even if they are party members, this does not considerably translate into local policy, including tax policy. This is a result, among other things, of the differentiation of the local government, where the different economic situations of municipalities make it challenging to implement a top-down policy on local taxes. Statements of the executive on this aspect are presented in Table 4.11.

Figures 4.18–4.20 show the results of questionnaire surveys of discussions about real estate tax rates. Tax rates were the least controversial topic

Table 4.11 Results of the focus study of the partisan political model

Partisan political model		
Aspect addressed	*Statement of the executive*	*Expected consequences*
Being a member of a party does not considerably translate into local policy, including local government tax policy (varying situation of the municipalities)	"I am not related to any party, I have never been a member of any party, and I do not represent the views of any party". "[...] to an extent, we have become politicians, but I have always tried not to be one and not feel one; I am not related to any party. For me, the most important thing is to [...] achieve what I have planned and what I believe is right for our development". "[...] the smaller the city, the less important your political affiliations are and the more important the person you vote for is, [...] the person you know from the street, from your neighbourhood, whom you know all about because it is hard not to know each other in small municipalities. The same is true of decisions, [...] which pertain to a given city, expectations of the residents, needs of the city, and often have little to do with the general policy or guidelines of specific political parties". "I am a party member, but first of all, I am a member of the local government here in the city. When I make decisions, not only tax decisions, I am guided by the best interest of my city [...]. I contact my fellow local government members more extensively, and my views [...] have never affected how I work here in the local government". "I make autonomous decisions with the Council, and party policy has no impact on that [...]. I have a lot of freedom in this regard". "[Fixing the tax rates] is different in every local government. It would even be hard to find a party suggestion or a direction in this regard. [...] Now, while such tax decisions are actually detached from the party directions, [...] the opposition committee [...] had the following slogan: "friendly tax policy", which should be plainly translated as "we never raise anything". Today, when good arguments are in short supply, they refer to that slogan as if there were no other arguments [...]. [...] this would make it very hard if the [...] party developed a sort of fiscal roadmap because local governments are so different [...] and it would not be applicable at all".	Political affiliations will be of no importance when decisions on tax policy are made.

Source: Own study.

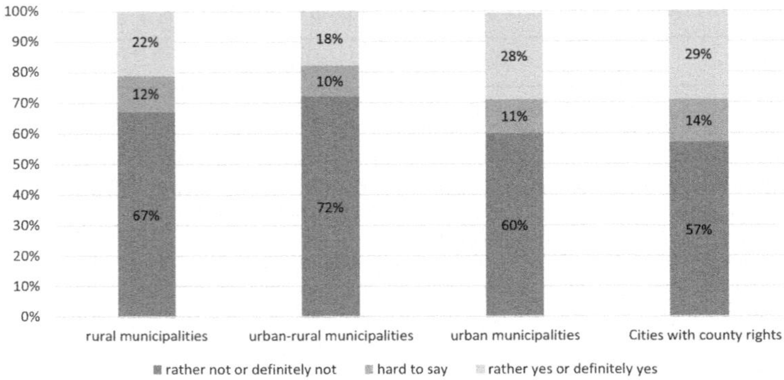

Figure 4.19 Were draft resolutions on real estate tax on buildings at their particular stages (initial draft, meeting of a competent commission, municipal council session) adopted in your municipality after a turbulent discussion?

Source: Own study based on survey data (municipalities).

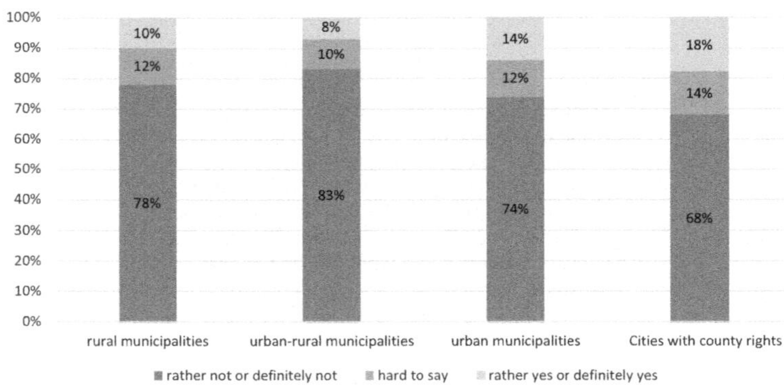

Figure 4.20 Were draft resolutions on real estate tax on structures at their particular stages (initial draft, meeting of a competent commission, municipal council session) adopted in your municipality after a turbulent discussion?

Source: Own study based on survey data (municipalities).

in urban-rural municipalities. Interestingly, buildings tax was discussed the most, while land or structures tax was less frequently mentioned.

The focus study proves that the level of identification with a particular political party at the level of municipalities is relatively low, meaning that the decisions made are primarily determined by the situation of a specific local government authority, only then followed by party ideology. Winning the required majority in the Municipality/City Council dominated by opposition representatives could be a problem because there is a temptation to build political capital on contesting decisions made by the executive, especially when a tax increase is at stake. However, contrary to expectations, tax rates are not the subject of a lively debate.

Bibliography

Alesina, Alberto, and Matteo Paradisi. 2017. "Political Budget Cycles: Evidence from Italian Cities." *Economics & Politics* 29 (2): 157–177. doi:10.1111/ecpo.12091.

Alesina, Alberto, Nouriel Roubini, and Gerald D. Cohen. 1997. *Political Cycles and the Macroeconomy*. Cambridge: MIT Press.

Black, Duncan. 1948. "On the Rationale of Group Decision-Making." *Journal of Political Economy* 56 (1): 23–34. doi:10.1086/256633.

da Fonseca, Mariana Lopes. 2020. "Lame Ducks and Local Fiscal Policy: Quasi-Experimental Evidence from Portugal." *Economic Journal* 130 (626): 511–533. doi:10.1093/ej/uez042.

Klien, Michael. 2015. "The Political Side of Public Utilities: How Opportunistic Behaviour and Yardstick Competition Shape Water Prices in Austria." *Papers in Regional Science* 94 (4). doi:10.1111/pirs.12101.

Łukomska, Julita, and Paweł Swianiewicz. 2015. *Polityka Podatkowa Władz Lokalnych w Polsce*. Warszawa: Municipium SA.

Piwowarski, Radosław. 2014. "Strategie wyborcze w świetle wybranych teoretycznych modeli głosowania." *Studia Prawno-Ekonomiczne* 93: 275–287.

Rogoff, Kenneth. 1990. "Equilibrium Political Budget Cycles." *American Economic Review* 80: 21–36.

Conclusions

This monograph presents the outcome of research on tax policies pursued by municipal governments in the countries applying mixed and area-based property taxation systems. Despite the prevalence of the area-based tax in some Central and Eastern European countries, real property taxes do not generally serve as a significant revenue source for local budgets, with Poland being an exception. Consequently, the analysis and examples primarily focus on Poland, emphasising real property tax as a pivotal aspect of local government revenue, with the assessment considering its specificity and significance in terms of the impact of municipal governments on productivity.

The multi-faceted character of this study is expressed in the course of considerations, including the theoretical frameworks of local tax policy, economic and legal assessments of real property taxation (including considerations of tax efficiency and justice, analyses of real property tax frameworks in Poland, and selected Central and Eastern Europe countries), and in-depth exploration of the tax policies implemented by Polish municipal management.

The first chapter of the monograph highlights local tax policy as a crucial tool of socio-economic policy, involving the necessity for local authorities to establish, for instance, hierarchical objectives, methods, and instruments for their implementation. Beyond meeting municipality financial needs, measures implemented through local fiscal policy ensure funds are used to meet the statutory tasks of municipal management bodies. Moreover, along with its fiscal function, municipal management can employ tax policy tools to pursue various non-fiscal objectives, and local taxes should be used to favour and promote socio-economic development. This pursuit of autonomous tax policy is facilitated by the financial autonomy of municipalities and the related taxing power.

The chapter comprehensively analyses existing global research on local tax policy while noting that previous studies have addressed both classical tax competition (*tax mimicking*) and competition for political capital (*tax yardstick*) in local tax competition. Local tax competition and the political budget cycle are prevalent in most countries. Still, it is crucial to point out that the scale and intensity of these phenomena vary significantly due to differing

DOI: 10.4324/9781003530503-6

levels of economic development, revenue self-reliance, revenue structure, tax types, and the extent of taxing power. These observations are the basis for the research and analysis presented in subsequent chapters.

Real property taxes, certain theoretical aspects of which were discussed in Chapter 2 of the monograph, play a pivotal role in the tax system as complements to income taxes, tightening the tax system by levying taxes on real property assets, regardless of the source of the latter. Notably, the immovable nature of the taxable object is paramount in the context of tax policies pursued by local governments. Because of a relatively stable tax base, real property taxes provide a steady revenue source for local communities. This monograph section delineates the current state of theoretical research regarding the effects of the real property tax burden. Also, it outlines the most significant theories of real property taxation, notably highlighting two distinct perspectives: the benefit perspective, which views local real property tax as payment for local public services (benefit tax), and the new perspective, which considers local real property tax as a distortionary tax on capital use within the local jurisdiction (distortionary capital tax). It also presents vital advancements in research on the effects of real property tax.

The approaches adopted by the European Union countries regarding real property tax exhibit diversity, with Western European nations predominantly adopting a real property value-based system, but challenges in determining actual property values often necessitate the implementation (or postulating) of changes. In contrast, the Visegrad countries are instead associated with the area-based approach. However, as detailed in Chapter 3 of the monograph, they also incorporate elements of *ad valorem* taxation alongside area-based systems, rendering their approaches mixed. Czechia and Slovakia show limited interest in transitioning to value-based taxation, notably due to the associated costs of establishing and updating cadastral systems, while in Hungary, local authorities retain the discretion to choose between land tax and construction tax systems. Challenges in determining the adjusted fair market value result in only a few municipalities opting for taxation based on such a value, with others resorting to the area-based system. In Poland, real property tax is calculated based on the area of land and buildings. In contrast, buildings rely on the value determined for taxation purposes, which typically differs from the market value. Romania stands out among the countries examined from outside the Visegrad Group, with a real property tax system often viewed as complex, non-transparent, unjust, and susceptible to manipulation, although also including elements that objectively differentiate the revenue potential of local governments.

Generally, in countries primarily using the area-based system, the efficiency of the real property tax tends to be lower than that of those employing *ad valorem* taxation. However, it is essential to note that the tax base is not the sole factor influencing the revenue generated for local budgets from this tax. The degree of taxing power holds significant importance in countries employing mixed systems, showing considerable variation in the analysed countries, as indicated in Chapter 3 of the monograph. In Poland, municipalities exercise taxing power chiefly by setting tax rates within statutory limits. However, the fiscal impact of this mechanism varies based on the taxable object, municipality type, and application timing. Although the basic tax rates are legislatively defined in Czechia, they are subject to adjustment through various coefficients, some affected by location or taxable object characteristics, while others hinge on the municipality. At the same time, Slovakian local government units serve as tax administrators, with the ability to modify land valuation for land tax. Moreover, Slovakian municipalities can increase or decrease real property tax rates within statutory limits and implement additional exemptions or reductions. The taxing power of Romanian municipalities primarily revolves around partial autonomy in setting tax rates, selecting the base value and granting established tax preferences. It also falls under the jurisdiction of local governments to index the base amounts of the tax according to the inflation rate. In Hungary, municipalities serve as the local tax authorities responsible for real property tax administration and also have the discretion to decide whether to implement the tax as well as determine the choice of the tax base, which can be either the area in square metres (land/utility) or the adjusted market value. However, it is essential to note that the rights given to local governments do not determine how much they will use their powers in their tax policy, ultimately affecting the revenue generated from real property taxation.

This monograph contributes significantly to the advancement of knowledge in the field of local government finance across various domains. Notably, it addresses the cognitive gap concerning tax policy at the local level, particularly considering the scarcity of European studies mentioned in the introduction. An innovative aspect of the work lies in the analyses conducted in Chapter 4, which explores the motives behind municipal tax policy. This study is one of the first comprehensive examinations of this sort of local tax policy to date.

The analyses in Poland reveal a correlation between the reduction of upper real property tax rates and municipality own revenue in the subsequent year. However, several key factors influence this correlation's strength, including the taxpayer's legal personality, municipality type, and geographical location. The presented analyses do not qualify to draw definite conclusions regarding the cause-and-effect relation or precise assessment of the factors' impact on revenue increase. The interdependencies are not explicit, and the very phenomenon is multi-dimensional. However, the conducted tests let us identify the determinants of the analysed phenomenon and highlight their statistically significant impact on the national scale, paving the way for more detailed multivariate analyses.

Furthermore, relationships between established tax rates and average rates in neighbouring municipalities have been confirmed, suggesting the presence of tax competition, wherein municipalities adjust their tax policies in response to activities undertaken by neighbouring municipalities within their taxing power. The strength of the relationships varies in real property taxes, although the analysis is based solely on the 2020 data. Despite this limitation, statistical tests on all municipalities in the country unveil statistically significant correlations, indicating their non-randomness, even when the correlation coefficient value is minimal. The strongest correlation ($\rho = 0.66$) was observed for the real property tax sections about business-related buildings, with notable variations contingent on municipal location emerging as a crucial determinant of tax competition occurrence. However, a comprehensive understanding of this issue necessitates extending analyses over a longer period, surpassing the assumed scope of this monograph.

Furthermore, the research indicates that real property tax increases are generally unpopular among residents, even if not substantially burdensome to household budgets. While local government representatives recognise the unpopularity of such decisions, the research proves that they strongly emphasise educational efforts to highlight the benefits of higher taxes to residents when faced with tax increases. The research findings do not support the presence of a median voter phenomenon. Despite local governments' awareness of voter preferences, which generally disapprove of high taxation, governments often fail to follow these preferences, mainly because real property tax does not significantly burden taxpayers.

Regarding the existence of a political business cycle, the study indicates a limited willingness to raise tax rates as the next elections are approaching, albeit the opinions of local government representatives on this matter remain ambiguous. Similarly, like with the concept of the median voter, this ambiguity is likely to arise from the perception that both municipalities and residents do not view real property tax as a significant concern. Furthermore, the level of tax rates does not significantly influence electoral decisions.

Additionally, local government representatives unanimously assert that, at the local level, they prioritise the needs of municipalities and residents over the political demands of their respective parties, meaning that the party model impact cannot be proven to exist at the local government level.

In conclusion, the local government policy exhibits specific distinctive characteristics. Primarily, it operates less on the party model; at the local level, where the authorities are closer to the voter, the needs of individuals count more. It is crucial to acknowledge that decisions concerning tax rates constitute a vital aspect of such local governance, and despite real property tax typically posing modest tax burdens, particularly for individuals, decisions to raise tax rates are generally met with disfavour. Nevertheless, research suggests that taxpayer preferences do not significantly impact decisions in this area, with educational initiatives playing a pivotal role here, illustrating the benefits of municipal actions to the residents, especially investments in social infrastructure. However, the proximity of the next elections does influence the inclination to raise tax rates to some degree – such decisions are approached more cautiously, particularly as political opponents can exploit them.

Annexe

Survey questionnaire (residents)

M1. Age:
☐ 18–24 yrs ☐ 25–34 yrs ☐ 35–44 yrs ☐ 45–54 yrs ☐ 55–64 yrs ☐ 65+

M2. Gender
☐ female ☐ male

M3. Education
☐ primary ☐ vocational ☐ secondary ☐ university level ☐ above university level

M4. Net income (take-home pay)
☐ up to PLN 2 100 ☐ between PLN 2 101 and 4 300 ☐ between PLN 4 301 and 8 600 ☐ between PLN 8 601 and 12 900 ☐ above PLN 12 900

M5. Municipality

M5.01. Municipality type (to be completed by the surveyor)

☐ city with county rights ☐ urban municipality ☐ urban-rural municipality ☐ rural municipality

M6. Voivodeship
Dolnośląskie ☐ Podkarpackie ☐ Kujawsko-Pomorskie ☐ Podlaskie ☐ Lubelskie ☐ Pomorskie ☐ Lubuskie ☐ Śląskie ☐ Łódzkie ☐ Świętokrzyskie ☐ Małopolskie ☐ Warmińsko-Mazurskie ☐ Mazowieckie ☐ Wielkopolskie ☐ Opolskie ☐ Zachodniopomorskie

M7. What is your primary source of income?
☐ employment contract ☐ contract of mandate/task-specific contract ☐ (disability) pension ☐ business operations

1. **Do you own real estate (land, buildings, homes)? If so, how many properties?**
☐ none ☐ yes, 1 property ☐ yes, 2 properties ☐ yes, 3 properties
☐ yes, more than 3 properties

2. **Do you pay real estate tax?**
☐ yes, as a natural person ☐ yes, as an entrepreneur ☐ yes, as a natural person and an entrepreneur ☐ I do not pay real estate tax

3. **In your opinion, the real estate tax burden for the residents of your municipality is:**
☐ very low ☐ low ☐ average ☐ high ☐ very high ☐ I do not know the real estate tax burden

4. **In your opinion, the tax burden for the entrepreneurs in your municipality is:**
☐ very low ☐ low ☐ average ☐ high ☐ very high ☐ I do not know the real estate tax burden

5. **In your opinion, should entrepreneurs and residents pay real estate tax at various rates?**
Rating scale: 1 – definitely not 2 – rather not 3 – hard to say 4 – rather yes 5 – definitely yes

a land

1 ☐ 2 ☐ 3 ☐ 4 ☐ 5 ☐

b buildings

1 ☐ 2 ☐ 3 ☐ 4 ☐ 5 ☐

6. **Should the real estate tax rate depend on (more than one answer):**
☐ the location (e.g. closer to or further from the city centre) ☐ the age of the buildings ☐ the technical condition of the buildings ☐ the type of use (e.g. residential or business) ☐ the type of development (e.g. single-family or multi-family) ☐ the value of the property ☐ the number of properties owned by the person or company

7. **To what degree may a lower real estate tax be, in your opinion:**
Rating scale: 1 - to a very low degree 2 - to a low degree 3 - to a medium degree 4 - to a high degree 5 - to a very high degree

a an incentive to form new businesses in the municipality

1 ☐ 2 ☐ 3 ☐ 4 ☐ 5 ☐

b an incentive to develop existing businesses in the municipality

1 ☐ 2 ☐ 3 ☐ 4 ☐ 5 ☐

c an incentive for residents to establish permanent residence

1 ☐ 2 ☐ 3 ☐ 4 ☐ 5 ☐

d a motivating factor for enhancing the financial well-being of the community

1 ☐ 2 ☐ 3 ☐ 4 ☐ 5 ☐

8. Should real estate taxes be:

☐ uniform country-wide
☐ varied across municipalities

9. Does municipal candidates' stated decrease/increase in real estate tax impact your decision to vote for them?

☐ yes, it does, the higher the taxes, the better ☐ yes, it does, the lower the taxes, the better ☐ maybe it does, the higher taxes, the better ☐ maybe, the lower the taxes, the better ☐ hard to say ☐ no, it does not

10. Would you be willing to change your place of residence or business to pay a lower real estate tax?

☐ place of residence
☐ place of business

Survey questionnaire (municipalities)

TERYT municipality code:...

Rural municipality	☐	Urban Municipality	☐
Urban-rural municipality	☐	City with county rights	☐

Please mark the appropriate with x. All the survey questions refer to 2020

1 Please rate municipalities' current degree of autonomy regarding tax-related power, explicitly referring to their ability to set real estate tax rates and adopt tax preferences.

Rating scale: 1 – very low 2 – low 3 – average 4 – high 5 – very high

1 ☐ 2 ☐ 3 ☐ 4 ☐ 5 ☐

2 In your opinion, are real estate taxes for entrepreneurs in your municipality:

Rating scale: 1 – very low 2 – low 3 – average 4 – high 5 – very high

1 ☐ 2 ☐ 3 ☐ 4 ☐ 5 ☐

3 In your opinion, are real estate taxes for residents in your municipality:

Rating scale: 1 – very low 2 – low 3 – average 4 – high 5 – very high

1 ☐ 2 ☐ 3 ☐ 4 ☐ 5 ☐

4 is it reasonable to vary real estate tax rates concerning taxpayer category (legal persons and natural persons) for the enumerated taxable objects?

Rating scale: 1 – definitely not 2 – rather not 3 – hard to say 4 – rather yes 5 – definitely yes

e land

1 ☐ 2 ☐ 3 ☐ 4 ☐ 5 ☐

f buildings

1 ☐ 2 ☐ 3 ☐ 4 ☐ 5 ☐

g structures

1 ☐ 2 ☐ 3 ☐ 4 ☐ 5 ☐

5 If the municipal council has varied real estate tax rates relating to land, which criteria were considered?

a location	legal persons	☐	natural persons	☐
b business type	legal persons	☐	natural persons	☐
c type of development	legal persons	☐	natural persons	☐
d purpose and use of the land	legal persons	☐	natural persons	☐

6 If the municipal council has varied real estate tax rates relating to buildings, which criteria were considered?

a location	legal persons	☐	natural persons	☐
b business type	legal persons	☐	natural persons	☐
c type of development	legal persons	☐	natural persons	☐
d technical condition	legal persons	☐	natural persons	☐
e age of the buildings	legal persons	☐	natural persons	☐
f business type	legal persons	☐	natural persons	☐

7 Which criteria were considered if the municipal council has varied real estate tax rates relating to structures?

a business type	legal persons	☐	natural persons	☐

8 Please rate the influence of the following factors on implementing real estate tax preferences in your municipality, including reductions, differentiation of tax rates, and tax reliefs and exemptions.

Rating scale: 1 – very low 2 – low 3 – average 4 – high 5 – very high

a an incentive to run a business there

1 ☐ 2 ☐ 3 ☐ 4 ☐ 5 ☐

b an incentive to develop entrepreneurship in the municipality

1 ☐ 2 ☐ 3 ☐ 4 ☐ 5 ☐

c an incentive for residents to establish permanent residence

1 ☐ 2 ☐ 3 ☐ 4 ☐ 5 ☐

d enhancing the financial well-being of the community

1 ☐ 2 ☐ 3 ☐ 4 ☐ 5 ☐

e higher budget revenue from real estate tax in the future

1 ☐ 2 ☐ 3 ☐ 4 ☐ 5 ☐

f higher budget revenue from PIT and CIT in the future

1 ☐ 2 ☐ 3 ☐ 4 ☐ 5 ☐

9 How do the rates adopted in neighbouring municipalities affect tax rate decisions?

	real estate tax for legal persons	real estate tax for natural persons
a rates in neighbouring municipalities influence rate reductions	☐	☐
b rates in neighbouring municipalities influence rate increases	☐	☐
c rates in neighbouring municipalities do not affect rates	☐	☐

10 In your opinion, are the objectives that justify the structure of the tax resolutions (such as tax rates and the introduction of subject-based exemptions) being implemented?

Rating scale: 1 – definitely not 2 – rather not 3 – hard to say 4 – rather yes 5 – definitely yes

a tax objectives

1 ☐ 2 ☐ 3 ☐ 4 ☐ 5 ☐

b incentive objectives for businesses

1 ☐ 2 ☐ 3 ☐ 4 ☐ 5 ☐

c incentive objectives for residents

1 ☐ 2 ☐ 3 ☐ 4 ☐ 5 ☐

11 Were the draft real estate tax resolutions in your municipality adopted following intense discussions during various phases, including the preliminary draft, committee meetings, and deliberations of the municipal council?

Rating scale: 1 – definitely not 2 – rather not 3 – hard to say 4 – rather yes 5 – definitely yes

a for land tax

1 ☐ 2 ☐ 3 ☐ 4 ☐ 5 ☐

b for tax on buildings

1 ☐ 2 ☐ 3 ☐ 4 ☐ 5 ☐

c for tax on structures

1 ☐ 2 ☐ 3 ☐ 4 ☐ 5 ☐

12 In your opinion, regarding real estate tax, should municipalities have the power (without statutory restrictions) to determine independently:

a individual types of taxable objects	YES	☐	NO	☐
b rates	YES	☐	NO	☐
c tax reliefs and exemptions	YES	☐	NO	☐

13 In your municipality, were there cases where councillor groups submitted motions to amend specific tax rates within the draft resolution on the real estate tax?

	land	buildings	structures
a yes, there were cases of motions to increase rates	☐	☐	☐
b yes, there were cases of motions to reduce rates	☐	☐	☐
c yes, there were cases of motions to both reduce and increase rates	☐	☐	☐
d no, there were no motions	☐	☐	☐

14 Is it more problematic for your municipality to collect PIT or CIT?
Rating scale: 0 – no problem 1 – comparable problem 2 – more problematic for CIT 3 – more problematic for PIT

0 ☐ 1 ☐ 2 ☐ 3 ☐

15 In your opinion, does the electoral cycle influence the likelihood of municipal councils making unpopular decisions regarding real estate tax rates?
Rating scale: 1 – definitely not 2 – rather not 3 – hard to say 4 – rather yes 5 – definitely yes

1 ☐ 2 ☐ 3 ☐ 4 ☐ 5 ☐

16 If reforms were planned regarding the powers of authorities, who, in your opinion, should be responsible for setting the real estate tax rates for the tax year?
Rating scale: 1 – municipality council, by a resolution 2 – town/city mayor, by an order 3 – province governor 4 – minster of finance 5 – hard to say

1 ☐ 2 ☐ 3 ☐ 4 ☐ 5 ☐

17 Would it be desirable to reform the structure of the real estate tax in Poland?

Rating scale: 1 – definitely not 2 – rather not 3 – hard to say 4 – rather yes 5 – definitely yes

1 ☐ 2 ☐ 3 ☐ 4 ☐ 5 ☐

18 Which real estate tax structure solution is fairer: based on property value or a tax levied on property area?

Rating scale: 1 – both are equal 2 – value-based tax 3 – area-based tax 4 – hard to say

1 ☐ 2 ☐ 3 ☐ 4 ☐ 5 ☐

19 Which real estate tax structure solution enables higher budget revenue: a tax based on property value or a tax levied on property area?

Rating scale: 1 – both are equal 2 – value-based tax 3 – area-based tax 4 – hard to say

1 ☐ 2 ☐ 3 ☐ 4 ☐ 5 ☐

20 If the value-based real estate tax formula is adopted, the tax base should be determined based on:

a cadastral value ☐

b market value ☐

c rental value ☐

21 Please specify the order of your association with the term "cadastral tax":

Rating scale: 1 – the least significant 2 – important 3 – the most important 4 – hard to say

a a disaster tax, indicating an additional, heavier burden on property owners

1 ☐ 2 ☐ 3 ☐ 4 ☐ 5 ☐

b a socially just tax, distinguishing the taxation of property owners based on their property's value

1 ☐ 2 ☐ 3 ☐ 4 ☐ 5 ☐

c an effective and stable real estate taxation system enhances residents' quality of life and promotes sustainable local development.

1 ☐ 2 ☐ 3 ☐ 4 ☐ 5 ☐

d a contemporary property taxation system, a model observed in developed EU countries

1 ☐ 2 ☐ 3 ☐ 4 ☐ 5 ☐

For Product Safety Concerns and Information please contact our EU representative GPSR@taylorandfrancis.com Taylor & Francis Verlag GmbH, Kaufingerstraße 24, 80331 München, Germany

Printed and bound by CPI Group (UK) Ltd, Croydon, CR0 4YY
14/09/2026
02216223-0005